INDY 500
✦ An American Icon ✦

by Julie A. Studer

Published & distributed by:
  Julie A. Studer

in association with:
  IBJ Book Publishing
  41 E. Washington St., Suite 200
  Indianapolis, IN 46204
  www.ibjbp.com

Copyright © 2010 by Julie A. Studer.
ALL RIGHTS RESERVED. No part of this book may be reproduced in any manner without the express written consent of the publisher. All inquiries should be made to Julie A. Studer at www.indy500anamericanicon.com.

ISBN 978-1-934922-19-4
First Edition

Printed in the United States of America

TABLE OF CONTENTS

Chapter One 1	Chapter Twenty-One 75
Chapter Two 5	Chapter Twenty-Two 77
Chapter Three 9	Chapter Twenty-Three 79
Chapter Four 13	Chapter Twenty-Four 83
Chapter Five 17	Chapter Twenty-Five 87
Chapter Six 21	Chapter Twenty-Six 91
Chapter Seven 25	Chapter Twenty-Seven 95
Chapter Eight 29	Chapter Twenty-Eight 99
Chapter Nine 33	Chapter Twenty-Nine 101
Chapter Ten 37	Chapter Thirty 105
Chapter Eleven 41	Chapter Thirty-One 107
Chapter Twelve 45	Chapter Thirty-Two 111
Chapter Thirteen 49	Chapter Thirty-Three 115
Chapter Fourteen 53	Chapter Thirty-Four 119
Chapter Fifteen 55	Chapter Thirty-Five 123
Chapter Sixteen 57	Chapter Thirty-Six 127
Chapter Seventeen 61	Chapter Thirty-Seven 129
Chapter Eighteen 65	Chapter Thirty-Eight 133
Chapter Nineteen 69	Chapter Thirty-Nine 137
Chapter Twenty 73	

The content for this book came from myriad sources including public media, personal opinion of racing associates, fans and industry sources.

Efforts have been made to verify dates and factual information. The book was written for fan enjoyment out of appreciation for the tradition and the sport.

CHAPTER ONE

Each year under an Indiana sky, 33 of the fastest drivers on earth strap themselves into missiles that propel them around a 2.5 mile racetrack at 200+ mph. They compete for a place in history and the coveted Borg-Warner Trophy, which is awarded to the best performer in this field – the man or woman who crosses the finish line first after 500 miles of mind-numbing concentration and raw bravado.

When Ray Harroun, driving the Marmon "Wasp," won the inaugural Indianapolis 500 nearly one hundred years ago, little could he have known then that he was being inducted into one of motorsports' most highly esteemed clubs, a small, revered sect of performers tested and proven at the top of their class and sport. To win "Indy" is to carve one's name in the stone of time. It is equivalent to finding the Holy Grail. The Indianapolis Motor Speedway now hosts the biggest one-day sporting event in the world, with more than 300,000 attendees making an annual pilgrimage to the track each May.

Walking through the gates of the Indianapolis Motor Speedway is like walking into a cathedral. Everyone remembers the first time he/she entered these hallowed grounds. The place has a soul. And somewhere beneath the veneer of grandstands, office buildings and garages beats a heart that echoes the greatest moments that happened here – the sounds and visions of races past – agonies of defeat and ground-swelling cheers of victory. Listen, you can hear it. Close your eyes, you can see it. Like an old wartime battlefield, this place captures and embraces history vividly. Heroes from the past, no longer with us, look down smiling. It is here that their true resting place lies. Their spirits live on and continue to move us.

Many, for whom auto racing is a religion, worship their gods here. And those gods seemingly perform miracles. In the face of often incredible odds, we've witnessed remarkable achievements. This place can be unsympathetic and unforgiving, trying the mettle of the sport's top performers. Yet treat the place with kindness and respect, embrace it and learn its ways; it will return such studied consideration by revealing its unique nuances. Just don't take it for granted.

Indy 500: An American Icon attempts to convey the day-to-day atmosphere, emotions, and frustrations of some of the key players – those of drivers, team owners, crew members and officials against the backdrop of unfolding events leading up to the big Sunday race during the Memorial Day weekend.

Providing an introspective look at how it all happens – the plans, schemes, ideas and dreams that put drivers into cars and those cars onto the track – we'll peek into the closets and crevices of the IndyCar fraternity as it prepares for the year's greatest race. And we'll explore the challenges that confront everyone on this quest for greatness.

The personalities coloring this world are numerous. Each year, they appear at the speedway to either relive past glories or strive anew for a taste of beckoning victory. Many of these individuals still possess the physical and emotional scars left by previous attempts. Winning is the goal, but for most, just *being* here means something special. Results aside, it's a race they will never forget.

Chapter One

Every year, there are a thousand stories to be told at Indianapolis – those of courage, tenacity, ambition, rivalry, injury and heartbreak. There are also tales of success, achievement, heroism and personal victory. As we move into another month of May, there are many more stories to be written. They are here, waiting to be shared. Hopes will be dashed, dreams broken, fortunes won or lost. As we celebrate victory, perhaps our winner will be joined in spirit by some of those heroes from races past. When it's all over and the crowds have diminished, this man or woman will silently reflect upon the hard work, people and preparations that helped make this greatest day possible.

CHAPTER TWO

Georgetown Road runs north to south along the western side of the Indianapolis Motor Speedway. At the 16th Street intersection, on the southwest corner, where you can choose to either head east into downtown Indianapolis, west along Crawfordsville Road, or progress down 16th Street into the suburb of Speedway, you'll find the main gate to 'The Brickyard,' this most famous of motor racing circuits. Nestled in the corner, next to a small tree-lined parking lot, are the speedway offices, in an attractive yet unobtrusive building from which this goliath of sporting properties is organized and managed.

Indianapolis embraces the Indy 500 like a young co-ed preparing for a big dance. Each May this young lady dresses carefully, smoothes her hair, then steps out to party like there is no tomorrow. And everyone is invited to join the festivities.

This particular May approaches in the wake of recent economic challenges, both within the United States and beyond. This industrial city of almost two million people was built over the years primarily upon the hard work and sweat of auto workers and farm laborers, yet resources over the past couple of years have been particularly tight. Manufacturers and businesses continue to contend with fallout from one of the worst economic downturns in over fifty years. Few people have been spared; skyrocketing personal and corporate debt, unemployment, bankruptcies, foreclosures and tightened bank lending practices have challenged discretionary spending and the availability of funds in nearly every sector. As costs of living spiral upward, we wonder who will turn out for this year's celebration. At times like these, will people be willing to lose themselves in sport?

Yes, they will. The response should not surprise us. American optimism and the human spirit do not like to be held down for long.

What better way for people to set aside their own troubles than to attach their hopes to the striving of rising stars? Twenty-first century sports offer some respite from everyday struggles, diversion from bad news and activities.

Perhaps we are attracted to the Super Bowl, Kentucky Derby, Wimbledon and the Indianapolis 500 because we love to be reminded of true human potential. We admire striving for greatness. In days when shareholder values and corporate greed often drive business decisions, and political idealism takes a backseat to bipartisan and special interest agendas, we find ourselves looking outward for inspiration, people to admire, achievements to applaud. We need heroes to remind us just what can be accomplished when vision, talent and hard work meet opportunity. We are ushered in to share this with them, to partake of something greater than ourselves.

In fact, the Indianapolis 500 field promises to be stronger than it has been in quite some time, with a field of around 40 cars vying for entry. How can this be? The third year of unified IndyCar racing after 15 years of contentious rivalry between competing leagues now draws the best teams and drivers – at last, everyone is pulling in the same direction.

In 2010, a brand new CEO with a strong marketing background and

Chapter Two

communications ties has taken position at The Indy Racing League, and IndyCar exposure and promotions seem to be taking shape for their strongest thrust yet. IZOD, a reputable, visible affiliate with solid funding and marketing potential, is newly in place as an enthusiastic title sponsor for the IndyCar series. This will be the eighth year of use for the current Dallara-based chassis; many teams have had time to purchase these models – in many instances, multiples. With new chassis designs under consideration for across-the-field implementation in 2012, the best time to use existing equipment is *now*.

CHAPTER THREE

Tim Northcutt, Indianapolis native, associate director of communications for the Indianapolis Symphony Orchestra, open-wheel racing enthusiast and regular Indy 500 attendee has missed only five of these landmark races since 1967.

Some of his favorite aspects of the Indy 500 include the pageantry and tradition of the events, the celebration's lasting one month long, and the excitement one feels as cars speed by at about 233 mph (at one time up to about 240 mph). He notes that Indy is the only race in the world in which cars awash in multiple colors line up three abreast in eleven rows to proceed down the track. He fondly recalls people on their feet, waving and cheering, feeling the energy-charged atmosphere of the crowd, Jim Nabors singing *Back Home Again in Indiana*, the invocation – a blessing given in the native tongue of each driver represented, Mari Hulman George calling out, "*Ladies and Gentlemen, start your engines,*" and the timing of the whole program being perfectly synchronized to not miss a beat.

Northcutt recalls how people loved to hear former broadcaster Tom Carnegie announce new speed records set on Pole Day. "All the big guns were out there, gaining massive publicity for the two weeks leading up to the race."

Bump Day was particularly exciting – and *so* tense. He remembers watching the anguish on the face of William Leonard "Billy" Boat in 2001 and 2002, as for two years in a row, Boat anxiously waited on the bubble as the slowest qualifier. In 2001, he survived 12 unsuccessful qualifying attempts by eight drivers in the last 48 minutes of the day. In 2002, he was the slowest qualifier and just made the cut. Says Northcutt, "This event is so competitive. If your wheels are still rolling when the gun is fired officially ending Bump Day, you are still eligible to finish your requisite four laps (a driver's time is determined by the average of these four laps) to potentially qualify."

Steeped in the grandeur of Indy's race events, his annual trek to the track with friends is loaded with memories.

"The night before the 1977 Indy 500, I graduated with 700 classmates from high school, and our own version of celebrating this milestone was to leave directly for Falcon Drive following the ceremony. Throughout my high school and college years, one of my closest childhood friends, Steve Gootee, and I would organize the Race Day experience that we shared with two-dozen friends, and we had it down to a science. It was so well planned that our pals dubbed it "The Gootee-Northcutt Race Day Extravaganza."

The "Extravaganza" crew was in fine spirits all night and the entire next day and we saw history in the making as A.J. Foyt became the first four-time winner of the Indy 500. When the checkered flag waved, hundreds of drunken crazies started jumping over the spectator fences and running toward the track to cheer for Foyt as he went by on his Victory Lap. The "Yellow Shirts" (speedway security forces) were scrambling to catch them, but they were hopelessly outnumbered. Foyt must've crossed the finish line on fumes, because his car ran out of gas and coasted into the third turn, where the drunks mobbed his car and began to push him. While the Yellow

Chapter Three

Shirts were chasing them, we (in our rather inebriated state from partying all night and day) decided this was the chance of a lifetime. I ran out to the apron of the track, knelt down, put my hands on the hot asphalt and grabbed a piece of melted tire rubber as a souvenir. As I began to stand up, I saw a Yellow Shirt running toward me and I shouted, "I just wanted to feel this historic moment, so I can tell my kids about it someday. I'm leaving." To my surprise, he stopped, smiled and pointed toward the spectator fence. I could tell by his expression that he felt the same way. On that day, we were kindred spirits."

While Northcutt has attended many races, he recalls each one. Some of the more exciting on-track moments he has witnessed include:

2006 – The Andrettis had had horrendous luck at Indy so far. Though Mario might have won three times, he had secured only one victory, in 1969. Michael had come close to winning several times. In the 2006 race, coming out of a caution flag with just 10 laps left, the Andrettis had their cars in the 1, 2, 3 and 4 positions. Michael was leading the race and his son Marco was second. Going into Turn 3, Sam Hornish, Jr. was bearing down on Marco and tried to pass, but Marco shut him down. Hornish had to back off to avoid colliding with Marco, resulting in Hornish's dropping back 10-12 car lengths. With the finish looming near, it seemed unlikely that he might regain momentum. But he did! In the middle of the backstretch, in less than one lap, Hornish ate up this difference and on the front straightaway of the final lap of the race, he passed Marco! Sam Hornish, Jr. pushed forward to win the 2006 Indy 500 by one car length – the second closest finish in the great race's history.

1982 – Gordon Johncock drove for Pat Patrick and was racing against Rick Mears. Johncock took and held the lead for the last 40 laps of the race, but for the last 20 laps, he and Mears raced wheel-to-wheel, battling all the way to the finish. Johncock pulled ahead to win. Yet, after 500 miles of hard racing, it was only one-and-a-half car lengths that separated first place from second.

1992 – The weather was so cold – 50 degrees – and it had been raining most of the weekend. It was the only time the track sold more hot chocolate than beer. Tires had difficulty heating up, many cars spun out. Scott Goodyear started last, 33rd, and raced all the way up to second place. Goodyear was gaining steadily on Al Unser, Jr., but simply ran out of real estate. Had the race been 100 yards further, he would have passed Unser to be the only driver ever to come from last place to first and win the race.

2005 – This was Danica's first Indy 500. In lap 55, the race leaders shuffled as a result of needed pit stops, and Danica assumed the lead on lap 56, marking the first time in Indy 500 history that a female driver had led a lap in competition. Later, on lap 155, a caution was drawing to a close when Danica initiated contact with other drivers, tangled up her own car, damaged its nose, and found that she happened to be in an advantageous location for quickly ducking into the pit for repairs. One more quick pit stop under a caution flag on lap 159 permitted her to change tires and top off her fuel. She gained valuable time by this, as the race leaders still needed to pit and fuel one last time. On lap 172, she momentarily took the lead again and held it for 13 laps before Dan Wheldon passed her. The finish line loomed near. With 10 laps left in the race, Danica passed Wheldon and *again* assumed the lead. The crowd went wild. Was the Indy 500 about to be won by the first woman ever? Wheldon caught Danica with about 6 laps left and ultimately won the race and the 2005 IndyCar Series Championship. Yet this young woman had had an incredible run (her final position – fourth place) and had fired the excitement of spectators who knew they were witnessing history in the making.

Wherever Indy 500 fans reside and whichever races they've witnessed, every one of them has favorite remembrances.

CHAPTER FOUR

Tony George was upset. For some time now, the Indy 500 had been a part of the CART (Championship Auto Racing Teams)/ Champ Car Series, but ongoing bickering and disarray within that organization now seemed to threaten the stability of the program itself. CART's flagship event was the Indianapolis 500 and George, owner of the Indianapolis Motor Speedway, began to feel that the objectives of the CART Board were not compatible with his own vision of the direction in which IndyCar racing should go. In 1994, he pulled out, formed his own series, The Indy Racing League (IRL) and announced that beginning in 1996, The Indianapolis 500 would be a part of this new series. All teams/drivers were invited to participate, but entry parameters would be determined in accordance with George's terms.

CART was up in arms. The organization responded by boycotting the legendary race and instead established its own event on the same day – The U.S. 500 at Michigan International Speedway. The CART race, though televised, failed to gain traction as a respected alternative to the established benchmark, tradition and grandeur of the Indianapolis 500. Simultaneously, the Indianapolis 500 was underway with 33 relatively unknown drivers participating. This race was won by Buddy Lazier, who drove a car for Ron Hemelgarn, a long-time bastion of the speedway. Lazier and Hemelgarn came away that day as Indy 500 winners. It seemed, however, that fewer people were interested in what was happening up the road in Michigan.

While still the people's preferred race, even the Indy 500 was failing to drum up the usual accolades that year. After what became known as The Split, open-wheel racing had divided and entrenched itself in two camps – both, it seemed – at the mercy of people not particularly in the habit of giving way. Without top teams and drivers participating across this new divide, the race's representative value seemed lessened, downgraded. Many hardened race fans didn't care much for what the race had become.

But George never underestimated the value of his own asset – he was certain that The Indianapolis 500 was the foundation upon which his series would succeed. He surmised that without this race, CART would likely flounder while the IRL would only increase in strength and credibility. Achieving this probably took longer and a more circular route than George had initially projected, but in the long run, the IRL was the last organization standing.

CART (Champ Car post-2005) did struggle and would eventually fall. Contributing to this would be a lack of growth-oriented/risk-taking leadership and decisive management. Eventually, even the rich kids on the CART block could – and would – only support it for so long. In the early 2000's, the top two teams in the CART stable (owned by Roger Penske and Chip Ganassi) stepped around the organization's boycott by entering the Indianapolis 500. Over the next few seasons, other CART teams followed their lead. By the end of 2007, faced with mounting costs, losses and dwindling fields of competitors, CART crumbled, closed up shop and sold the majority of its assets to the IRL.

Twelve years following the acrimonious split, open-wheel racing would be once again on track. The strength factor in George's plan had worked as

Chapter Four

predicted. As to whether or not the Indy Racing League's credibility was increased, opinions are mixed. The split was ultimately a disaster which inflicted injury upon multiple parties, distracted key players and diminished the sport's overall potential. Even today, two years after reuniting, some of those individuals continue to grapple with the ramifications of that 11-year separation.

In retrospect, perhaps George had foreseen what would be the inevitable consequences of CART's chosen direction. At one time, it had been a powerful and popular series, but it also possessed a number of internal fissures that would have eventually cracked open the organization's façade; weaknesses that, with or without the split, would have eventually challenged CART's long-term success.

Concerns had grown over mounting costs of racing, and because the CART organization had been influenced by the special interests of its own teams, and team interests had taken precedence over series administration as a whole, CART lacked the decisive leadership that might have led it to the public popularity and commercial effectiveness that racing entity NASCAR enjoys. CART needed clear leadership, but because the influence of individual teams was so strong, the organization functioned more democratically, as a response to interests and wants than directorially, proactively advancing a specific vision mandated by decisive leadership. It found itself, like its drivers, going around in circles.

The IRL had secured in Tony George a benevolent dictator who saw it his responsibility to protect the heritage of the Indianapolis 500 and guarantee the racetrack's continued growth as a sporting property. Confident that his direction should honor the destiny of the Indianapolis Motor Speedway, he would promote his vision while upholding the interests of the IMS family business and standing firm against external parties threatening his turf. And if mounting a competitive challenge to CART was to result in the latter's eventual fall – then that just might have to happen.

CHAPTER FIVE

In the early 1990s, CART had seemed to be flourishing, having built considerable momentum over the previous decade. The number and strength of participants had been impressive; the field had been competitive. The series continued expanding into new venues and it appeared to many that a stock market flotation would guarantee the series additional financial stability and continued growth.

Ironically, the discrepancies CART had had with its predecessor league were not unlike the discomfort Tony George was having with CART. Many viewed George's breakaway action as similar to that of team owners in 1978 who had split off from USAC in order to form CART. The reason for that original split had also centered around team members disagreeing with the direction in which the series was moving and their feeling powerless to influence or stop it. When USAC resisted imparting greater control to team owners, the latter quit the league and formed their own sanctioning body, Championship Auto Racing Teams (CART).

The new CART principals were issued ownership of their own series, complete with a Board of Directors comprised of team owners and significant auto-racing figures, which would eventually come to include Tony George, president of the Indianapolis Motor Speedway.

The USAC continued to race. The formation of CART ushered in a period in which two separate series competed against each other; a situation to be later replicated between CART and the IRL. USAC races decreased in popularity just as CART races began appealing to a whole new generation of race fans. With fast cars that were exciting to watch, these bore many similarities to Formula One racing. The drivers, many of whom had established their reputations at Indianapolis, had begun to become household names: Gordon Johncock –winner of the first CART race in Phoenix, Mario Andretti, Al Unser, Bobby Rahal, Danny Sullivan and Rick Mears – the first CART champion.

Different chassis constructors were invited to compete together with engine manufacturers who would bring credibility and sustainability to this new series. As CART increased its profile, attracting sponsors, gaining media coverage and diversifying its races across a spectrum of oval, road and street courses, American open-wheel racing finally seemed to be on course to meet CART leaders' expectations for stability and financial growth.

So what went wrong within the CART organization that caused Tony George to depart? Group deficiencies in planning and strategy seemed to be problematic factors, and a perceived predilection to arrogance would further alienate less influential members of the series. The fundamental failure of the CART model might inevitably be credited to managerial and maintenance tendencies superseding entrepreneurial instincts for growth –opportunity-seeking, risk-taking and series development/expansion.

From the early days of CART, continuing through the leadership of John Capels, Bill Stokkan, Andrew Craig and Joe Heitzler, corporate sustenance and governance seemed a greater priority than independent ideas and growth. CART's leaders held their positions tenuously, by the approval of the organization's board. With many powerful personalities influencing each decision and with so many of these characters either pursuing independent agendas or being at odds with each other, it seemed only a matter of time before the organization stagnated. With Tony George's resignation from the board and subsequent announcement of going it alone, CART suddenly found itself in a different position.

If CART members wished to race at Indy, they were being asked to join the Indy Racing League, which meant denying CART sole series supremacy. Though CART members might have entered cars in the transitional 1996 Indy 500 (functioning with existing specs), they instead chose to go to Michigan and implement their own counter-event.

The prevailing perception in auto racing was that the U.S. could not sustain two separate open-wheel racing series; there did not seem to be sufficient distinction between them to make supporting both reasonable. Rather than capitalizing upon unique branding, a reactionary CART adopted the IRL's lead, matching its ideas and schedule rather than asserting its own value and brand. CART had its jewels. Road and street courses had provided excellent competition and were well-supported by both sponsors and fans. Long Beach had always been a popular venue and the appeal of racing on southern California's coast still carried the organization's profile high. Additionally, CART had name races established in respected locations. It seemed less concerned about the external threat that a start-up competitive series would provide.

Yet the Indy Racing League had become an *itch* that CART couldn't scratch. Pride was on the line and no one was willing to be viewed as the lesser entity. In response to IRL's creation, CART management might have stepped forward to proactively assert authority as the established auto racing organization. Instead, it waited for the IRL to act. If the IRL zigged, CART zagged; whether purposeful or not, CART did not wish to be seen as stagnant. It seemed, however, that CART was overlooking its own valuable assets – the drivers, races and sponsors that made up its own series. It became more interested in beating Tony George than in further developing its own product or capitalizing upon its identity and advantage as the "established" open wheel series. Perhaps the organization would have fared better by focusing more upon its own unique character.

CHAPTER SIX

To many men, there is still something threatening about a woman in a racecar. They perceive it as inconceivable that she might outrace her male counterparts and view her audacity to try as an insult to masculinity. So when 23-year-old Danica Patrick led 19 laps at the speedway in her rookie appearance in 2005, then finished fourth, men scratched their heads in wonder. They scrutinized her thoroughly, looking for something to dislike about this 5'2" wisp of a girl who had cracked the rank of 200 mph racecar drivers. Had a female really just done this? How could she?

Danica was one of three women to be entered in the 2009 race and she achieved distinction beforehand as a favorite who might win. This stretched the imagination of the still male-dominated racing world. While Danica had won a titled IndyCar race in Japan in 2008, regrettably few people in the United States had witnessed it due to the timing and shortcomings of the race's broadcast. Danica now needed to capitalize upon that win by strengthening her resume upon U.S. tracks, satisfying the home crowd. What better place to do so than at Indianapolis?

Danica can be outspoken with opponents when she feels wronged. In a sport accustomed to seeing men express frustration by throwing off their helmets after a race and brawling, with voices raised or fists flying, throwing a woman into the mix confuses things. How dare she throw a tantrum. Do women do that? Just who does she think she is?

Danica *knows* who she is. Her confidence comes from a lifetime of racing, beginning in go-karts at a young age and working up the circuit from there. Measure her experience with that of her male contemporaries and she'll hold her own. Danica does not figure gender into her racing mindset, nor does she want or expect separate or special treatment. She is not out to make statements on behalf of the feminist cause. She just happens to be a woman in what has traditionally been a man's sport. She is simply focused upon doing what she does best; she wants to beat the guys at their own game on equal terms. She's done it before, she can do it again, and she knows it. So if onlookers perceive an air of arrogance, this may just be Danica forging her way through new territory, keeping her mind in the zone.

Like it or not, Danica has created a buzz that has proven exceptionally beneficial for auto racing in general and the IRL in particular. As a consequence of her success, she provides hope and motivation for thousands of other aspiring young women. As is common with celebrity, that Danica is petite, attractive, and not reluctant to capitalize upon her marketing appeal, has been helpful. This has enabled her to advance her image, broaden the diversity of the sport's fan base and draw greater public attention to IndyCar racing. Sponsors have approached her with a view toward reaching previously untapped demographics – those of youth and women.

While refining this combination of commercial aptitude and racecraft, Danica's racing personality and character continue to develop. Some might suggest that she is perpetually hard on herself, resulting in an impatience which could hinder optimal performance. She is not unaware of this. As her experience increases, so does her self-discipline and ability to rein in the

Chapter Six

exasperation that could frustrate situations and increase the risk of mistakes. Her career is still young, her focus forward, her potential strong. And there is much more work to be done. Danica Patrick *is* threatening in a race car, boys. That's just the way she likes it.

CHAPTER SEVEN

Driver Helio Castroneves, of *Dancing With the Stars* popularity, took his partner by the hand and led her through the moves that would together bring them victory. This formidable pairing of driver and race car executed a string of deft maneuvers, putting on a performance that would be applauded by all. In this, his first appearance on this stage, car and driver moved as one, maintained perfect rhythm throughout, capturing the hearts of fans and spectators as they took the checkered flag for a win. Dancing with thirty-two other stars, Castroneves won the 2001 Indianapolis 500 on his first attempt and repeated this victory in his sophomore race in 2002, establishing a solid reputation for speed and becoming a firm crowd favorite.

As the sweltering Florida summer of 2008 drew to a close, IndyCar racing's most colorful character reflected upon his achievements. Since his arrival in the United States from Sao Paulo, Brazil, he had evolved into something of a superstar. His talent, personality and charisma had opened doors that he had dared not believe possible. If people doubted that the American Dream was still within reach, they only needed to look at his impressive, progressive career path.

No one noticed dark clouds looming on the horizon. It is easy to imagine Castroneves being stunned by the drastic shift his life would take as Uncle Sam came knocking on his front door in the form of an IRS lawsuit.

Castroneves, his business manager and sister Kati Castroneves, and Alan Miller, his legal counsel, were charged with conspiracy and six counts of tax evasion for allegedly failing to report over $5 million dollars of income to the Internal Revenue Service between 1999 and 2004. Each count carried the penalty of a maximum five-year prison sentence. In early October, the three defendants surrendered to authorities. Helio Castoneves pleaded not guilty and was released on $10 million bail.

His world was at risk. A guilty verdict, he knew, would end his career. And so began the trial which would prove to encompass the longest days of his life.

Many racecar drivers characteristically need to exert control – not just on the track, but consistently throughout everyday living. While some may purport a more passive or mellow demeanor than others, beneath a calm exterior burns a cauldron of intense drive, independence and self-sufficiency, valuable ingredients of determined competitors who can seize the wheel of their own lives, advance at an unusually blinding pace and navigate around particularly dangerous obstacles in intense situations. Drivers need to be able to make their own calls, quickly and decisively without waiting for external input or feedback. Some manage this better than others. Even the most successful drivers experience meltdowns; these are often born of frustration, and ironically, may occur at those times when the control they crave lies within their grasp.

When any person is injured or sick, he often still feels that he possesses at least *some* resources at his disposal, some influence or maneuvering to secure a successful outcome, be it strength of mind, body or will. However, in Castroneves' situation, his future was placed into the hands of entities

Chapter Seven

unknown to him, of those unfamiliar with his character or behavior. These were not necessarily colleagues, friends or fans of the motor sports genre in which he had excelled. There was no sense of camaraderie here. He was at the mercy of other people who dictated all directives, terms and timing regarding this important personal matter which bore colossal professional ramifications. To be so far removed from his familiar surroundings and fully dependent upon the goodwill and judgment of strangers had to be highly unsettling.

The ensuing courtroom battle became more intense and emotionally draining than any competition Castroneves had encountered on a racetrack. In the midst of his stormy days of isolation, distress and despair, his faith, family and friends gathered near, provided refuge and ultimately bolstered his strength.

This time, there were no stylish strides with which to impress. His dancing partners had become the legal team representing him, headed by Miami attorney Roy Black. This judge and jury would not hold up scorecards, but would determine the course of his immediate future. If found guilty, he faced a possible sentence of up to 30 years in prison or at the very least, deportation.

CHAPTER EIGHT

Gerry Forsythe had done everything right. A CART team owner since 1983, the Illinois native was not a man to do anything halfway. In spite of early success with a number of highly-rated drivers, Forsythe sold his team in the mid 1980s to focus upon further developing *Indeck*, his energy business. He returned to racing in 1993, partnered with Barry Green to form Forsythe Green Racing, and initially competed in the Formula Atlantic Championship, a developmental series for aspiring CART drivers. The team joined CART in 1994 and added French-Canadian driver Jacques Villeneuve. They began to accumulate some impressive results.

The following year saw Green and Forsythe go separate ways, each taking ownership of an independent team. When Tony George introduced the Indy Racing League, Forsythe was instrumental in upholding the defense against the new series. He also became a leading figure in the plans to take CART stock public, a move designed to shore up the finances of the organization and raise funds to further expand the series – money that would be sorely needed in competing with a fortified contender.

Tony George directed the IRL autonomously; CART struggled amongst conflicting personalities and divisive management. As CART chairman Andrew Craig prepared a strategic plan, the CART board, which included owners Gerry Forsythe, Carl Haas, Roger Penske, Pat Patrick, Carl Hogan, Bobby Rahal, Derrick Walker and Chip Ganassi, pulled in multiple directions. Special (individualized) interests seemed to take precedence over cohesive organizational thinking, which, in turn, slowed the rate and probability of progress.

But one thing that CART possessed at this stage was equity, and equity still had value. The series continued to sustain a strong sponsor in PPG Industries. Contracts were still in place for popular races in venues ranging from Long Beach and Mid-Ohio to Toronto and Surfer's Paradise in Australia. A contingent of popular, successful champion drivers still attracted fans from overseas, as well as across the United States. TV ratings were still reasonably high and manufacturer interest in engine supply continued with the involvement of Mercedes-Benz, Toyota, Honda and Ford.

A business-savvy manager knows that equity and value can, with strategic planning and timely execution, be leveraged into sustained growth via investment and acquisition. Forsythe, among others, saw no reason why the CART organization should not continue to succeed and prosper. From a financial standpoint, a breakaway series would have a significant effect upon any valuation CART claimed. As CART's board members and management team prepared to take their stock public, they may have underestimated the threat that this new upstart posed to their personal stockholdings. This miscalculation would contribute to the dissent and acrimony amongst CART leadership that would eventually play into George's hands.

Though George had never closed the door on a solution, he was not willing to negotiate away the Indianapolis 500. As upset voices within the CART organization grew louder, they only served as provocation for him to continue down his own path. By now it was obvious that George's new league was actually beginning to come together. There would be two separate series

Chapter Eight

racing in 1996 and CART would be functioning without administration of its most significant event – the Indianapolis 500.

The IRL in those formative days was not without its own challenges. Both parties had underestimated the stubbornness of the other; neither would budge. George had gambled on at least two or three of the big teams shifting allegiance to the IRL, but this did not happen. CART counted on the IRL's failing and George's being forced into a compromise, but this did not come about, either.

As the 1996 season progressed, Andrew Craig and the CART board members began preparing for their stock market flotation. A substantial portion of the projected capital raised would be invested in developmental opportunities for up and coming drivers – specifically the Formula Atlantic Championship and Indy Lights series. Both entities had loyally supported CART for years. They would be used to nurture driver talent for the primary series and would also provide supporting races at all CART events. CART began organizing additional races to flesh out its calendar of events.

CHAPTER NINE

At the time that entries closed for the 2009 Indianapolis 500, there were 78 cars listed for 31 elected drivers representing 18 teams. The regular Indy Racing League teams were all present, some with additional entries for second or third drivers – and as was typical, there were several entries by smaller teams that race the Indy 500 as their *only* race of the season.

The expense of participating in this race is highly subjective; indeed, the cost of racing at all might necessitate a team's being ready to commit a blank check. An IRL chassis car currently runs $680,000 (including wiring and spooling) to assemble and enter; this does not figure in engine expenses. The IRL currently only uses engines supplied by Honda and these cannot be purchased; they must be leased. Different race package options are available, but the least expensive one covers one qualifying weekend in addition to the race event.

Other expenses include those of personnel, tool and equipment, spare parts and transportation for crew to and from the track. These are minimal expectations, essential coverages, and do not include the additional discretionary factors of hospitality, marketing, fundraising and use of a motor home during a team's stay at the track. When a team rounds out all the numbers, it can expect to spend close to $1 million to race in the Indy 500.

The big teams – the Penske, Ganassi and Andretti organizations – pay their drivers to race, or at least sponsors do, so one can add driver salaries to the expense list. Smaller teams will try to find those drivers who will attract sponsorship to offset this cost. In many cases, no money is exchanged between team and driver; a team will offer a drive to a suitable candidate with the hope that the driver's name and track record will be sufficiently lucrative to attract a good sponsor.

Many teams utilize substantial merchandising programs to supplement their budgets. For some teams, sales of T-shirts, baseball caps, jackets, etc. can often account for more than one-third of their total income.

Then there's prize money. Those teams able to finish in the top five or so on any consistent basis can win a substantial amount to put in the team's account.

Finally, there is the investment of personal resources from team owners, many of whom are successful businesspeople who have generated income from a variety of businesses, ranging from car dealerships and computers to health clubs and record labels. Smaller, part-time teams are far more dependent upon owner financing than are larger, full-time teams.

Traditionally, the small "Indy only" teams have, over the years, made up a significant portion of the 33-car field. What these team principals all have in common is a passion for racing and a dream that compels them to compete when the probability of a strong finish and top placement are minimal.

Each year, Indianapolis draws them back for another run, sometimes as if

Chapter Nine

common sense has been cast aside and the challenge has taken hold. Owner Ron Hemelgarn, a former Indy 500 winner, recalls how on many occasions he has vowed never to return because the expense of racing was so high. He admits that it takes strict discipline to not overstep one's prescribed budget. The secret is to know what a team can afford and under no circumstance exceed that amount. For Hemelgarn, who has raise his racing funds from the health club and fitness business, strict adherence to that cut-off point has been required for him to stay on the track and participate year after year.

By tradition, the Indianapolis 500 is limited to 33 starters. The Indy Racing League has only 20 or so regular entries, so to make up the numbers, the race needs to have a number of teams supplement their existing entries with additional cars and drivers. It also needs the annual attendance of small teams, who essentially spice up the competition through their one-off appearances.

Indianapolis is unique in that it is the car, not the driver, that guarantees a team's entry. Teams enter cars first and can nominate drivers at a later point. Many teams enter two cars per driver with one designated as a spare, in the event that an additional one is needed. So in seeing 78 cars entered in a race, one can reasonably expect that nearly half of the entries are spare cars and a small number of these are represented by teams who have yet to name a driver – hopefully one who will bring enough money or sponsorship to pay for his or her drive. Many small teams often *wing it*, first naming their driver, then hoping that funding can be secured on the basis of that driver's good practice and qualifying performance. Of course, this is something of a "catch-22" scenario. In order to successfully complete qualification, one must have funding, but in order to achieve funding, he first must qualify.

CHAPTER TEN

As Spring attempts to assert its presence at the Indianapolis Motor Speedway, the buds of May begin peeking through the leaves and clover around the perimeter of the track. Teams come from across America, drivers from all four corners of the globe, or sometimes both from just down the street. Competitors begin arriving at the speedway in good time to claim allotted spaces, set up equipment, and importantly these days, motor homes. Each team is assigned a workshop in the garage area.

There is an area to park the transporter – or *hauler* – the mobile engineering unit, space for one's hospitality unit, and a place for the requisite million dollar motor home or bus, presuming that a team possesses the resources for acquiring one. But such is the game of one-upmanship in this business that few self-respecting drivers or team owners will be without state-of-the-art living facilities. Borrowing or leasing is acceptable, but if one can help it, he avoids showing up short-handed.

There have usually been two or three races before May, so we are into a season that by that time, has already begun forming ideas about its winners, losers, favorites and also-rans. Gone are the days when competitors would be out racing regularly every week. Most drivers now focus upon only one championship, with the exception perhaps of the Sebring 12-Hour or Daytona 24-Hour races, both sufficiently prestigious for drawing the best drivers across the U.S. from all disciplines of motor sports. Years ago, when Indy was more in tune with grass-roots championships, some drivers had perhaps raced more than two dozen times before this point in May. It was more of a fulltime professional livelihood than an occasional event. They would come from stock cars, midget cars, sports cars, dirt races – you name it. Upon arrival, they would don crash helmets and driving gear, then jump in their cars for what used to be a full month of practice and qualifying.

But times have changed. When the Indy Racing League came into existence, the month of May still encompassed more than three weeks of driver and vehicle preparation activities, beginning with rookie orientation, then the official opening day on which cars took to the track for their first practice runs. In keeping with tradition – a concept invoked and revered as the situation suited – cars were on the track five days a week leading up to Pole Day, when the three fastest drivers qualified for the front row of the starting grid, locking in those slots which guarantee their initial positions for the race. The following week would involve five days of running in preparation for Bump Day – upon which teams learned if their cars had made one of the 33 possible slots or had been "bumped out" by faster vehicles. If one was ranked as the 33rd fastest, then a car clocked a time faster than his, the former would be bumped out. Each car could attempt to qualify three times before being eliminated. An unqualified driver was eligible to drive a qualified car and the driver who qualified it could be replaced if his team wished to do so. Slots near the bottom of the ranking were particularly precarious, as there would often be more than fifty cars competing for one of these 33 slots. This inevitably resulted in much tension and anticipation. Pole Day and Bump Day weekends were exciting events for spectators and those days would often draw crowds in excess of 200,000!

Today's vehicles are highly sensitive, so many variables beyond mechanical preparation come into play – track, weather, driver training, experience or handling of the vehicle, adjusting to developing situations, a driver's strategy vs. that of his competitors, etc. Just when a driver thinks he has it right, along comes a gust of wind, or track conditions shift, altering the handling characteristics of the car.

One will see confused looks and exasperation as well as much arm movement and facial contortion from a driver trying to best describe his vehicle's handling as he hustles it through the turns and down the straightaways. Another suggestion is made, a different adjustment, and the driver heads out for another drive. One lap, two, perhaps several, and the driver ducks back in again. The car is still not quick enough.

With each adjustment bringing continual incremental improvement, one would think that after ten days or so at the track, a car would eventually function at optimal performance. But no. Just when a team thinks it has the combination right, the weather or track surface changes, which may impact vehicle performance and require different settings; it could very well render the previous day's work useless.

So it goes. Teams spend days chasing their tails. With the cost per lap run at Indianapolis calculated at about $300-$400 each (not including damage expenses), it is easy to understand how two or three weeks of a car's work on the track can soak up about 20-30 percent of an entire annual budget.

CHAPTER ELEVEN

In 1996, Indianapolis had experienced an economic tsunami that washed over the entire region. Previous years had seen an upturn in business, commencing from the first week of May and culminating in an influx of nearly 500,000 people converging on the speedway over Memorial Day weekend. But not that year. Hotels reported that their business was down. Restaurants, gas stations, souvenir shops all wondered if they were victims of an unfortunate miscalculation. Attendance at the Indianapolis 500 was lower than usual, and though the speedway released no official figures, commentators and journalists noted that both racing constituents and the public seemed uncertain about how to perceive the new division created within open-wheel racing.

The organization of the IRL had been declared in 1994 and 1996 was to constitute its first racing season. It would be a building year for the IRL. With no star drivers represented and no particular mechanical improvements to the vehicles, that year's Indy 500 seemed to hold less allure than usual to participants and race fans. Several people felt that they had been cheated out of the event's full promise and potential.

But Tony George had a plan and was working it. He had introduced the Indy Racing League in large part to revise or correct the inequities he had perceived within the CART organization. Open-wheel racing had had multiple engine suppliers and the expense of racing for entrants had been driven higher and higher with commonly shifting machinery expectations. Wealthier CART owners were able to meet these, but smaller or part-time teams struggled. George sought to manage short-term costs by grandfathering-in the engines already in use (no initial changeover expense in transferring from CART to his league).

George suggested that costs would be better contained within his league, steering clear of the multi-million dollar budgets and runaway expenditures that had been affiliated with CART's financially secure participants. His emphasis would be on providing teams and drivers with an affordable racing alternative, which additionally provided entry opportunity into the Indy 500.

He also believed that the United States needed a series that drew its talent from the pool of American drivers who competed throughout the country in multiple grass roots racing categories. George wished to provide an affordable opportunity for them to compete in the top tiers of open-wheel racing – namely, the IndyCar Series and Indianapolis 500. American race fans indicated that they wished to see more American drivers participating, yet it seemed that these were fading farther and farther from the starting line-up. The Indy Racing League intended to once again place an emphasis upon American talent by drawing its entries from sprint and midget racers.

George also promoted making the IRL an all-oval series, in which each race, in essence, simulated the effect of racing a mini-Indy 500. This would help contain costs as vehicle set-ups for running on road surfaces differed from those designed for continually turning left on racing ovals.

By George's writing the rules, promoting the racing and overseeing the

Chapter Eleven

management of his own proprietary series, he believed that he could stave off any competing interests/agendas that he perceived as self-serving.

Tony George began planning his series in 1994, two years before the finished car concept came onto the scene. Beginning in 1997, the series would have its own chassis and engine package. Exclusive arrangements had been made with British racing car constructor G-Force and the Italian marque Dallara. Power would be provided by V8 Oldsmobile engines supplied by General Motors. The cost of a ready-to-race car would be in the region of $450,000, about half the expense of a CART package. This sounded good in theory, especially to small teams that might race only once a year – then, most likely in the Indy 500. For them, the expenses of outfitting a car had likely deterred a number of talented, would-be contenders. With Tony George responding supportively to their interests, their not being required to utilize the high-tech machinery necessary to be competitive in CART, and the costs of racing coming at a more affordable price tag overall, smaller teams now saw the IRL as an inclusive, attractive, affordable alternative to CART. Perhaps an Indy 500 win lay within their grasp, after all.

CHAPTER TWELVE

It would be challenging to convince the CART establishment, with its high-tech machinery and multi-million-dollar budgets, that the IRL was a worthy alternative. Importantly also, George and his public relations team would have to sell his argument to the fans, who valued watching top performers and did not, themselves, have to bear those costs which made racing either possible or prohibitive.

Significantly, in 1998, shortly after the forming of the IRL, CART had taken its stock public, raising $100 million in the offering. Many of the stockholders were team owners, protective of these investments, unwilling to see the value of their holdings decline. It would be unrealistic to think that owners would jump ship and work against their own investments, however George surmised that the Indy 500 carried substantial weight and that without it, CART's value would decline. He was correct. Faced with the prospects of lost prestige, value and income, CART's stockholders braced for turbulent days ahead.

Among the changes introduced by the IRL was a revised racing season schedule which would begin during the spring and climax with the Indy

500 as a grand finale in May. The great race's coming at the end of the season might generate further excitement if it just so happened to be the pivotal event in settling the series championship.

The proposed change that the CART organization probably found the most difficult to swallow was George's idea of awarding the top 25 starting positions to the top 25 drivers in the IRL championship. This would leave non-regulars to vie for simply the last eight remaining positions on the grid – few spots and the least advantageous starting points. CART perceived this as a measure designed to aggravate them and perhaps increase their teams' defection to the IRL. George's plan as presented, however, didn't work. Under fire without and within, his plan hit resistance; the blueprint had to be revised. It came to light that multiple commercial interests – the sponsors and media particularly – balked at a staggered calendar season, citing economic constraints and marketing challenges that would make such a change difficult to maneuver. The IRL withdrew the proposition and returned to the established model in use.

In hindsight, greater alliance-building within and without might have better prepared the IRL for the relationship alignment and commercial realities of those first years. Good market research and focus groups might have signaled to them just what team owners and drivers, race fans and commercial sports interests were prepared to accept. The careful, strategic timing of announcements, execution, and a delayed transition year might have alleviated confusion and helped grease the wheels of the IRL proposition, ensuring warmer reception.

CART fought back point for point, not ready to let a competitive series shake its market-dominant position. Following the Indy Racing League's announcement of its 1996 calendar, CART countered with an announcement of its own locations and dates, scheduling many to coincide with planned IRL events. The most significant calendar conflict was CART's introduction of the inaugural US500 race, to be staged at Michigan International

Chapter Twelve

Speedway on the same date as the Indianapolis 500. The response further fueled the fire between rival leagues. Both sides now entrenched, defended their positions, leaving the motor sports community at large displeased.

CHAPTER THIRTEEN

Roger Penske, the acknowledged "Captain" of auto-racing, sets the standard for amassing racing wins as a team owner. His team has achieved 319 major race wins, 149 specifically in Indy Car, including capturing the Indianapolis 500 15 times. Penske was a professional driver from 1958 to 1965, when he retired to pursue other interests, including auto team ownership. He was Sports Illustrated's driver of the year in 1961.

The brand Team Penske is synonymous with success in the Indianapolis 500. When one considers the effort, resources, skill, dedication and professionalism needed to win with this level of frequency and consistency, one begins to appreciate the caliber of talent, sport expertise and business knowledge that Roger Penske and his organization bring to the track. No other team comes close to this level of performance, and each year, he raises the bar further. Roger is a team owner who has recognized and capitalized upon the value of racing as a tremendous tool for business development; he has implemented this resource throughout his core activities away from the racetrack, as well.

Penske's diverse business holdings range from car dealerships, truck leasing and diesel engine manufacturing to Cars Direct, an Internet car sales venture; Universal Technical Institute, a national automotive engineering training facility; and Deer Valley, a world-class ski resort in Utah. He began Penske Racing in 1965, a logical extension of his automotive businesses, which had included buying and selling racecars.

While able to readily finance outstanding equipment and top talent through his multi-billion dollar Penske Corporation, there are several factors that set Roger Penske apart as a leader.

He leverages his reputation and success to generate continued goodwill and sponsorship through highly developed marketing, hospitality, and PR programs at the racetrack, particularly at Indianapolis. Centering around themes and campaigns that motivate employees and sponsors alike, he reaffirms alliances with the Penske brand and those businesses affiliated with it.

Drivers and staff members marvel at the depth of knowledge he possesses about his businesses, and the specificity of detail he puts forth. Penske knows what he is talking about. Believing that chance favors the prepared, he is highly strategic, anticipating situations, playing out possibilities and formulating contingency scenarios.

Contemporaries admire his character. While hard-working, determined, and driven to win, he is also revered by colleagues for honesty and follow-through on everything he says he will do.

An important component of Penske's top-notch operation involves taking good care of his people. He fosters a particularly strong loyalty amongst himself, drivers and crew. He understands the roles and value of those people who have made his operation successful and is renowned for upholding those who perform well for him.

Chapter Thirteen

When driver Rick Mears mangled both feet in an accident in 1984, Penske held his seat for him, and Mears returned to secure his fourth Indy 500 win under Team Penske.

Helio Castroneves' indictment and subsequent trial threatened to put sand in the well-oiled gearbox of his team's machine. In true form, however, Penske stood by his man and held his spot.

Castroneves' trial overlapped the start of the 2009 season which kicked off in St. Petersburg, FL. A short-term replacement driver was needed and the likeable, capable Australian, Will Power stepped in. No one, it seemed, would fail to take notice of a competitor whose name was *Will Power*. Following the wrap-up of CART activity, he seemed certainly experienced enough to fill Castroneves' shoes for the interim. Power would complement Penske's other regular driver, Ryan Briscoe. Both were proven race winners who demonstrated championship potential. Power had previously raced at Indy and should be able to deliver the requisite experience and attributes Roger Penske sought in a driver.

As Castroneves was occupied with legal business, Power began testing for Team Penske. He performed with the understanding that if Castroneves was acquitted, the latter would immediately return to the team and his lead seat, dropping Power to the slot of third driver. Even under a temporary arrangement, Power saw a great opportunity here. No driver would turn down the chance to drive for Team Penske. In the St. Petersburg Grand Prix on April 5th, the first race of the 2009 IndyCar Series, Will Power made his mark by finishing in a credible sixth place. The race was won by his teammate, Ryan Briscoe.

At the same time that the teams headed west for the series' second race at Long Beach, Castroneves' trial in Miami was finally winding down. The jury met behind locked doors. After seven weeks of anxious waiting, Castroneves would receive his verdict at last.

Real lessons in life occur when we are confronted with losing that which is most important to us. Castroneves had had plenty of time for intent reflection. The events of the past several months had challenged and exhausted him. There were times he was convinced he would never again sit in a racecar, when he was certain that the wellspring of opportunity he had discovered and nurtured had run dry. More importantly, there were moments when he feared that the people he cared for might soon be out of his reach. He worried for his sister Kati, and attorney Alan Miller, who were experiencing this nightmare themselves.

Out from behind the wheel and far from the track, he was disconnected from the venue and activities he'd known best. He hoped to awaken and find that this experience had been nothing more than a bad dream.

CHAPTER FOURTEEN

Springtime in Indianapolis brings forth a kaleidoscope of color; blooming trees permeate the many public parks downtown and in surrounding suburbs. Long-frozen ground softens and gives way. Doors burst open as people awakening from winter slumber scurry outdoors. The speedway stirs with renewed life. The air buzzes with energy, hope and anticipation as the countdown to race day begins.

The city itself has witnessed a major revitalization over the past decade or so. Areas that had once been *no man's land* now invite residents and visitors to come occupy the space and linger awhile. Restaurants, clubs, bars, museums, galleries and parks can now be found in abundance in locales which had, not many years ago, hosted broken-down warehouses, empty office buildings and boarded-up shop fronts. The real estate boom of the 1990's and early 2000's, as throughout most of the United States, had seen a proliferation of new housing and industry. Indianapolis had undergone cosmetic surgery to restore her aging beauty and with it, had given birth to an energy that embraced a new generation. In essence, Indianapolis had become cool again.

It bills itself as *The Racing Capital of the World*. Daytona, Monaco Silverstone and Le Mans might similarly lay claim to this, but certainly Indianapolis boasts the necessary credentials – it is home to a world-class track and the premier race by which open-wheel racing qualifies and acknowledges its top achievers. The expansion of NASCAR to the Indianapolis Motor Speedway in 1994 and on-again/off-again presence of Formula One racing over recent years further justify this claim. The track has hosted three titled races for each of these three distinct auto racing genres.

The French introduced auto racing by organizing the first Grand Prix. Since then, the United States has added its own unique take on the motor sport. European open-wheel racing has traditionally utilized road courses almost exclusively. By contrast, the United States, particularly the Midwest, has favored small oval tracks – some dirt, some paved. Both continents have blended these styles, however, oval track racing in Europe is still fairly new. It is only over the past 15 years that it has established a European presence and it is slowly gaining popularity. Racing sprint cars, those specifically designed for running on oval dirt or asphalt tracks, is a distinctly American car racing genre.

CHAPTER FIFTEEN

At one time, car racing was a means of experimenting with advanced technology and test-driving new auto systems and parts. Public highways had become insufficient and inappropriate platforms on which to try out the latest and increasingly faster automobiles of American car manufacturers. As many of these operations were headquartered in the Midwest, Indianapolis had become central to the engineering and development of automotive components and it was thus seen as a convenient and practical location at which to build a much-needed test track.

Local businessman Carl Fisher was the first to envision such a facility. Fisher had made his fortune producing headlamps for a variety of car makers through his Prest-O-Lite company. In 1906, he drew up plans for a track that would permit the unrestricted needs and unlimited speeds the manufacturers sought. It took some three years for his dream to be realized. He acquired 320 acres of farm land five miles northwest of the city and in 1909 began construction on what would become The Indianapolis Motor Speedway. His partners in this project were industry associates Arthur Newby, Frank Wheeler and James Allison.

The dimensions of the speedway today reflect its original layout – two parallel 5/8 mile straights and two 220-yard straights at the north and south ends. Connecting them are four turns measuring one-quarter mile each. The length of the track, one full lap, is two-and-half miles.

The first 16-race weekend in August of 1909, became something of a disaster following bad weather and deteriorating track conditions. There were several accidents, and five people were killed, including one driver, two riding mechanics and two spectators. The final race was stopped before its conclusion.

The track surface required reinforcement with more suitable materials than the original crushed stone and tar. The automotive racing program was postponed for the resurfacing to occur. While consideration was given to other materials, brick pavers became the element of choice. These were able to form a solid base which had proven effective on local highways in neighboring states. The track surface, completed in 1909, was comprised of 3.2 million pavers. *The Brickyard* was born. Subsequent races verified the relative safety and sturdiness of this new base. Though the track would eventually be covered by a hot mix asphalt which remains in use today, three feet of brick pavers still remain exposed at the start/finish line as a tribute to the traditional surface.

The track gained notoriety and enthusiasts soon envisioned its hosting a grand event that would test the mettle of the fastest performance cars and best drivers over a demanding distance of 500 miles. The speedway was up to the challenge, and on May 30, 1911, the Indianapolis 500, "The Greatest Spectacle in Racing," was born.

CHAPTER SIXTEEN

Seventeen days after Bob Sweikert won the 1955 Indianapolis 500, two 15 year-old Italian boys stood on the dockside in New York City, soaking in the sights and sounds of the new world into which they had just arrived. The Andretti brothers, Mario and Aldo, began racing stock cars at the local short track of Nazareth, the small Pennsylvania town that had become their home. These kids had been inspired by their Italian hero, Alberto Ascari, who ironically was killed at Monza in Italy only days before the family left for the United States.

"It could have been either one of us," Mario admits. A coin toss had determined that Aldo would be the brother to premiere the family's home-built Hudson Hornet in its first race in 1959. But later that year, an injury as the result of a serious accident would temporarily sideline Aldo's racecar driving career. Brother Mario persisted and would come to win more than 20 races in his first two seasons.

Mario began laying the groundwork for an impressive career within open-wheeled race vehicles, occasionally extending his reach into Formula One racing and stock cars. In 1967, he won the Daytona 500. He would subsequently win four IndyCar championships, as well as the 24 Hours of Daytona, 12 Hours of Sebring (three times), the USAC National Championship (dirt track), International Race of Champions, Formula One World Championship and Indianapolis 500.

In 1969, the year of Mario's Indy 500 triumph, Aldo Andretti was again victim to a horrendous accident when, in a sprint race at Des Moines, IA, he crashed heavily into a fence and incurred severe facial injuries which brought his racing aspirations to a definitive close.

Mario and Aldo Andretti each fathered offspring who would replicate their achievements, perpetuating legacies set in motion by their fathers and establishing a family motor sporting dynasty that continues to thrive. Michael Andretti, Mario's son, began racing IndyCars similarly to his father. John Andretti, Aldo's son also took the IndyCar path, coupled with a stint in stock cars. Michael's brother, Jeff Andretti, raced IndyCars until an injury suffered at Indianapolis ended his career. Michael's son, Marco has become a regular driver in the IndyCar series.

Over the course of his career, Mario drove for a variety of different teams. One of these included Newman-Haas (now Newman/Haas/ Lanigan), a team originally assembled by racecar importer and impresario Carl Haas. Haas had enticed actor Paul Newman into partnership after promising to secure Mario Andretti to be the team's driver. At the time, Haas had no assurance that Mario would agree to this arrangement, but via the sheer power of persuasion and possibility, Mario did accept the offered drive. Victories and championships followed for this winning combination. Mario's son, Michael, eventually joined the Newman-Haas team and an Andretti powerhouse ensued.

These developments preceded the now infamous split. Newman-Haas had become a regular contender in the CART championship, however when the Indy Racing League set up shop in 1996, Paul Newman, as a Newman-

Chapter Sixteen

Haas principal, particularly felt betrayed by its departure from CART. He was among the leading forces behind the Indy boycott and was very vocal in his opinions against Tony George and the IRL.

Mario and Michael remained loyal to their team throughout this period, but over time, as CART began showing signs of weakness and the IRL continued to gain momentum, drivers began to miss competing in the Indy 500. The Indianapolis 500 began to miss the caliber of drivers rendered unavailable since the split. It was obvious that the two camps had reached an impasse. Mario, one of the sport's elder statesmen, was called upon to bring some common sense to the table. He, among other respected racing influentials, mediated between the divided factions, attempting to bring both sides to agreement. American open-wheel racing was wasting away and as the principals on both sides refused to budge, stubbornness, ego and pride appeared to be significant obstacles to resolution.

CHAPTER SEVENTEEN

Heading one of IndyCar racing's most successful teams, both in CART and the Indy Racing League, Chip Ganassi has guided his team with steely determination and unwavering focus. When Floyd 'Chip' Ganassi began his IndyCar team in 1990, he did so with one goal – winning.

He had tasted victory at Indianapolis one year before as part-owner of Emerson Fittipaldi's winning car and after finishing first in the championship later that same year, parted ways with his driver, Pat Patrick, to begin his own team. As a former driver, Ganassi had competed in five Indy 500s between 1982 and 1986, but a serious crash in Michigan, during which his car spun off in a series of pirouettes, reinforced his notion that perhaps it was time for him to achieve success from the other side of the fence.

As a team owner, Ganassi set his sights on beating the best in the business: Roger Penske. To gain the edge he would need, he proved that he was prepared to take risks. British company Reynard Motorsports, at one time the world's largest racing car manufacturer, entered CART in 1994, back in the days when the series carried multiple chassis and engine manufacturers throughout any given season.

Forward-thinking Ganassi, fascinated by the artistry of racing, and eager to live on the cutting edge of innovation and technological development, spotted opportunity to implement an advantage. He entered two of Adrian Reynard's latest untried machines. Reynard Racing Cars had an enviable reputation for being ultra-competitive and had won first time out in every category they'd entered.

Ganassi Racing was thriving. Michael Andretti won the first race of the year at Surfer's Paradise in Australia. Then followed four consecutive CART championships from 1996 to 1999, with drivers Jimmy Vasser, Alex Zanardi (twice) and Juan Pablo Montoya. In 2000, the Ganassi team would set the ball rolling by becoming the first team to break ranks with CART and enter the Indy 500 with cars for Montoya and Vasser.

Juan Pablo Montoya dominated the race. For many at this time, his victory drive home fueled the argument that CART had superior drivers, that Indy Racing League entries were essentially second-tier competitors, and that the Indy 500 had become an inconsequential race in the overall scheme of things. Since the inception of the IRL and the division of the two series, the Indianapolis 500 had witnessed a significant drop in both attendance and TV ratings. Without star names, those drivers who had long held the imaginations of the racing public, and importantly, the interests of sponsors, the IRL seemed to be struggling to establish initial respectability. By the same token, CART, now lacking a flagship race, was having difficulty maintaining its profile as the United States' preeminent open-wheel racing series.

Tony George's initial gamble that the best teams from the opposing series would quickly switch their allegiances from CART to the IRL had fallen short. Marketing attempts to attract new teams to the series by offering a guaranteed start in the Indy 500 went unheeded.

Chapter Seventeen

Initially, the first 25 starting spots in the Indy 500 would be reserved exclusively for Indy Racing League members. CART perceived this as greater insult than incentive for them to join. George could keep his series, and without them, the largely devalued Indianapolis 500 would become worth even less, they argued. But, George surmised that without the Indy 500, CART's product offering would be less substantive and decidedly less attractive. Both assumptions were correct. Someone had to budge. Putting commercial consideration above personal ego, Chip Ganassi made the first move.

At the time of starting his first team in 1990, Ganassi had begun what has become one of the most successful and enduring team/sponsor relationships in motor sporting history. The combination of retail giant Target stores' enthusiastic, innovative marketing programs with Ganassi's on-track success created a formidable commercial partnership that continues to this day – *Target Team Chip Ganassi*.

Unlike Team Penske, which was only one of Roger Penske's many multi-million dollar companies, Ganassi's operation was more or less his principal business. Unlike many other teams on the circuit who were limited to much smaller outfits, Ganassi's organization was growing in multi-dimensional proportions and would include NASCAR and Grand Am Sports Car Series teams. The business had been built on the passion of a racer, but was run on common sense business principles.

One that Ganassi embraced was that of watching out for the interests of his business partners. After several years of commitment to CART, and with little to no progress being made in the open-wheel standoff, Ganassi took a long, hard look at his team's position and determined how best to move forward. Indianapolis was still a sponsor's dream destination and Target wanted to be at Indianapolis. After an absence of five years from the Indianapolis 500, Target Team Chip Ganassi blazed the trail home.

CHAPTER EIGHTEEN

At the time Roger Penske and Chip Ganassi entered the Indianapolis 500 and broke ranks with CART, another of its leading teams, Team Green, was not far behind. Owners Barry and Kim Green had achieved considerable success over recent years, and had won the Indianapolis 500 and CART championship with French-Canadian driver Jacques Villeneuve in 1995, the year before the series split.

Once this occurred, Team Green continued its CART affiliation for several additional years, but it was inevitably unable to ignore the commercial value of competing in the Indy 500. In 2002, Team Green stepped across the boycott, entering cars in the Indy 500 for its drivers Canadian Paul Tracy and Scotsman Dario Franchitti.

That year's Indy 500 result and subsequent fallout inflicted bad feelings throughout IndyCar racing for some time to come. On the final lap of the race, Helio Castroneves had been leading. An accident on the track brought out yellow caution flags – directing drivers to slow down and not overtake other cars – just as Paul Tracy was in the process of overtaking Castroneves. Tracy crossed the finish line in first place and the crowd cheered his triumph.

But the win was contested. IRL officials ruled that Tracy's pass had not been completed until *after* the yellow flag had been posted. Tracy was thereby awarded second place, and Castroneves was declared the victor.

Thousands of people in the stands and millions of viewers watching on TV had witnessed the pass. In reviewing video footage afterward, many questioned the judgment of the officials who responded with certainty that they had made the correct decision. Continued replays showed Tracy passing Castroneves within those controversial moments. In taped footage, where viewers struggled to see yellow lights displayed until moments following the pass, there was less satisfaction with the IRL ruling. Undeterred, the Indy Racing League declared that the last lap of the race would not count. The result would be finalized based upon the positions held at the conclusion of lap 199.

Many people felt cheated. Castroneves, together with his Penske crew, scaled the fence in front of the grandstand in their traditional *victory climb*. Paul Tracy's heartbreak turned to anger.

As did Barry Green's. This was not *just another race*. This was the Indianapolis 500! Green scrambled for the rulebook. He cited regulations that he was convinced would prove his point, but as his post-race appeal moved through the hierarchy of the IRL, he felt that his arguments were falling upon deaf ears. The appeal process would not achieve resolution for an additional five weeks and would cost Green a considerable sum in legal fees. Midstream, Green thought he heard that he was being denied permission to appeal. Overall, it had served to be a frustrating, confusing process that eventually upheld the original IRL ruling and left bad feelings all around.

Tony George, the IRL's president, had made a firm decision in the rare instance that such a victory might be challenged. Having exhausted all avenues of protest, Team Green returned to the CART series in disgust, vowing never to return to Indy.

Chapter Eighteen

Barry Green was done. Following the IRL's official ruling, he sold his shares in Team Green to Michael Andretti. For some time, Andretti had been operating a *satellite team*, Team Motorola, with Barry's sister, Kim; the Andretti/Green model had already shown itself to be an effective partnership. Michael and Kim reorganized the group and Andretti Green Racing Team* was born.

By this time, CART was sinking fast, losing sponsors, teams, drivers and races. With the Indianapolis 500 as its anchor, the Indy Racing League had been able to build credibility for top auto racing performance. It gained a reputation for its races being fast and close. The recent migration of Penske Racing and Ganassi Racing had included enlisting their star drivers, which strengthened their position and appeal to other IndyCar racing entities. At last, the IRL had surpassed CART as the more commercially viable series.

A decisive vote was cast in 2003, when the Andretti-Green team announced that it would enter the Indy Racing League. Driver Paul Tracy elected to remain in CART, which still reeled from losing his win at the Indianapolis 500. Following the Indy 500 in 2003, Michael Andretti wound down his driving career and opened a new chapter in the Andretti family saga, that of pursuing success as a team owner.

---

* In late 2009, Kim Green sold her shares in Andretti-Green Racing Team. The team has been restructured and renamed Andretti Autosport.

CHAPTER NINETEEN

From the days of the gang of four who developed the speedway together, owners and promoters have had to carefully balance the needs of competitors, manufacturers and teams with the insatiable hunger of fans for an exciting race and ongoing entertainment on race day. Also requiring consideration have been the interests of performers: drivers who have put their lives on the line while striving to fulfill their own sense of destiny – a shot at immortality. Over time, economic and political issues have regularly come into play, as well. A succession of owners have had to find and maintain a fine balance amongst these diversified, often competing interests and priorities.

From the P.T. Barnum-esque showmanship of those early years, the speedway has witnessed management styles that have reflected the often flamboyant personalities of owners and associates, from Carl Fisher to flying ace Eddie Rickenbacker and the illustrious Wilbur Shaw. But it was in 1946 that Terre Haute businessman Anthony Hulman would purchase the track and lay the foundations of what we see today.

As the landscape of the United States continued to change, transforming into the automotive and industrial powerhouse of the world, auto racing became a mirror through which manufacturers could reflect their innovation and expertise. Increasingly, racing was used for both technical development and marketing. Success at such high-profile events as the Indianapolis 500 guaranteed carmakers the image and credibility that they believed would boost sales.

The Indianapolis Motor Speedway was initially built as a testing ground and development facility for newly-established auto manufacturers to sample new ideas and improve existing technology. Over time, auto manufacturing supplanted experimentation. The track was no longer needed for its original purpose. The Indianapolis 500 became the venue's primary source of revenue. For eleven months of the year, the track lay quiet, awaiting the annual return of the racing circus. Successive decades saw the *modus operandi* shift due to simple necessity. The track lay quiet throughout WWII and fell into disrepair. In 1946, Tony Hulman, at the urging of three-time Indy 500 winner Wilbur Shaw, stepped in to save the facility. He purchased and refurbished the track, making numerous improvements.

That Hulman and his team were able to stage an event in 1946 was testament to his vision and determination. And race that year they did. Under his watchful eye, the "greatest spectacle in sports" was able to experience a rebirth that nurtured a new generation of enthusiasts and ushered in family leadership that would direct the speedway's operations for the next 64-plus years.

Up to, and including, the CART years, the speedway had been infamous for its competition between car manufacturers, in particular, the smaller specialist race car constructors. Through the days of the Duesenbergs, Studebakers, Hudsons, Tuckers and Novis, to the thunderous roadsters of the fifties and rear-engine machines of the sixties, with their innovative and often flamboyant designers or owners, racing cars continued to evolve. The Duesenberg brothers, Preston Tucker, Harry Miller, A.J. Watson, Smokey

Chapter Nineteen

Yunick, and Colin Chapman each put their unique contributions into racing car development. The ongoing rivalry amongst these *outlaws of speed* only added to their interest. Those were different days then. Oldtimers still reminisce about the camaraderie, competition and thrill of it all. Like pilgrims drawn to a holy site, they still come, the anticipation and hope are still there. Nothing can keep them away.

CHAPTER TWENTY

An Indianapolis native who has attended the Indy 500 from a very early age, Brian Barnhart has long-standing ties to the speedway and its flagship race. He has worked for a number of race teams and served in multiple positions, including working on the pit crew of Al Unser, Jr.'s winning car in 1992. Any sentimentality he may feel for this community is understandable. He is keeper of the flame and has to keep it burning. Barnhart's breadth of experience, teamed with a practical, cautious nature and good instincts, equips him for knowledgeable, thoughtful responsivity to problem-solving, both within the corporate office and at the track.

Barnhart wears many hats. As Chief Operating Officer for the IRL, his job includes overseeing on-track competition for the league, in addition to managing many of the elements that, behind the scenes, determine the policies, strategies and actions designed to ensure the continued stability, growth, and ultimately, the survival of the sport. In addition to dispensing official duties, he also fills the unofficial roles of cheerleader, caretaker, and often, judge and jury.

Add the responsibility of *safeguard* to that list. Barnhart holds the unenviable position of determining when to postpone a race in the interest of securing appropriate track conditions. The first two races of the 2010 season underwent heavy rains shortly before and during the races (Sao Paulo and St. Petersburg). In spite of disrupting carefully choreographed programs and risking the logistical nightmare of displacing sponsors, media and fans, Barnhart both times made the decision to clear the track and await safer conditions. In the instance of Sao Paulo, a slick street surface also caused Barnhart to postpone driver qualification the day before until the surface could be improved. Drivers and teams understood that these decisions had not come lightly; they were outspoken in their appreciation of Barnhart's protection of their safety.

CHAPTER TWENTY-ONE

To make a small fortune in racing, so the saying goes, *one best begin with a large one.* There are many who, from their own racing experience, would agree with this axiom. The sport will quickly suck dry the resources of even the wealthiest contenders if spending is not kept in check. When Anton "Tony" Hulman bought the speedway in 1946, he had the backing of his family business to help mobilize, then sustain the track through lean times and expansion or improvement periods. The Hulman Company had been established in nearby Terre Haute for nearly one hundred years at that time, and had earned a solid reputation in the grocery and provision business, in particular, with its *Clabber Girl* baking soda brand.

Wilbur Shaw operated the speedway until his 1954 death in a plane crash. Tony Hulman took the reins at that time and shortly thereafter became recognized as the *de facto* face of the Indianapolis 500. Hulman made his mark on the sport by sustaining and renovating the speedway, earning the gratitude of both participants and fans.

Hulman held diversified business interests, including real estate, utility companies and media outlets, however, it was the speedway which was closest to his heart. He was shrewd enough to recognize that it would not be a self-supporting entity and unless it secured the assistance of mainstream revenue sources, it would struggle to stay afloat long-term. Hulman never viewed the speedway as a profit center, but was rather committed to upholding the Indianapolis 500 and its reputation as the pinnacle of American motor sporting events. Upon Hulman's death in 1977, the race was sustaining regular attendance of over 400,000 spectators on race day, with a worldwide audience of more than 100 million TV viewers in over 50 countries.

Following Hulman's death, long-time Hulman Company executive Joe Cloutier stepped in as president of both The Hulman Company and the Indianapolis Motor Speedway. He presided over several significant challenges, including the team owners' dispute with USAC in 1978, which resulted in the formation of CART. Over the next 12 years, under Cloutier's leadership, the speedway would undergo extensive renovation and the race would experience a steep increase in prize monies awarded. This, combined with the growing popularity of pre-split CART, helped guarantee the ongoing prestige and glowing reputation of the Indy 500. Joe Cloutier died in December of 1989, but his office was not vacant for long. Tony Hulman's grandson, Anton Hulman "Tony" George, would preside over the operation of the business for the next two decades and would implement his own vision for the future. Taking quick, decisive action, he announced plans that would influence major changes at the speedway and would ultimately resound loudly throughout the motor sporting world.

CHAPTER TWENTY-TWO

Tim Cindric looked at his watch. The affable president of Penske Racing was awaiting news of his star driver's fate. Days had passed and the jury in Helio Castroneves' trial was still deliberating 3,000 miles away in Miami. Here in Long Beach, CA, there was a race to be run. Will Power ignored the distractions around him. As Castroneves' stand-in, he knew that the return of the favorite son could limit his long-term tenure with Team Penske. Not knowing what the coming days held for him, he savored his driving opportunities moment-to-moment.

The verdict was announced and cheers burst out within the courtroom. Though the jury remained hung on one count, Helio Castroneves had been determined "not guilty" on all others. At the conclusion of six months of preparation, seven weeks of trial and six long days of jury deliberation, Helio Castroneves stepped out onto Flagler Street a free man. With no more tears left to shed and the last hug given, he reached for his cell phone. Three thousand miles away in California, Team Penske's Tim Cindric answered. Helio Castroneves was back in business.

CHAPTER TWENTY-THREE

That one single sporting event has had such an influence upon an entire community speaks volumes for the importance of this single race. Even if attendee turnout has shown some decline in recent years, the enduring reputation of the Indianapolis 500 continues to belie pundits who suggest that the race has seen its best days. Under the auspices of the United States Auto Club (USAC), created by the late Tony Hulman as the sanctioning body for the Indianapolis 500, and under the watchful eye of Tony George and now new CEO Randy Bernard, the Indy 500 race event has continued to prosper. Successive decades have witnessed progressive growth in the quantity and quality of entries, number of spectators and both national and international media coverage.

Even if there had been no split, and CART had continued to hold sway as the unchallenged racing league, one considers how the race might have persisted or changed over time. Key factors impacting this include sustenance of the local economy, technological development, standardization of racing rules, differences in leagues' organizational governance, the rise of competitive entities and differences in branding and marketing.

For more than four decades, from the 1950s through the 1980s, the race event had drawn the attention of a worldwide audience. As it had grown in stature, so too had the reputation of Indianapolis as a center for the auto-racing industry. And with this had come the growth of peripheral businesses serving the profession. Racecar constructors, racing teams, engineers and an abundance of supporting suppliers had infused the Indianapolis economy, establishing the roots of a motor sporting industry that provided tangible benefits to the speedway and surrounding community. Speedway operations had brought and sustained industry-related jobs to the region in a timely way. The IMS had come into its own at the same time that many original car companies and manufacturers, once the local economy's mainstay, finally closed or relocated out of the area. What developed in Indianapolis and its surrounding geography was an innovative technological and creative collaborative culture of auto, speed, mechanical and manufacturing experts – strong feeder conduits for competitive motor sports.

The mechanics and art of auto-racing also continue to evolve. As the sport progresses throughout the 21st century, so must it adapt to the developing, shifting nuances of technology, entertainment and business. Speeds can only increase until they become too dangerous, costs can only increase to the point of becoming prohibitive, and open-wheel designs are limited by the constraints of what constitutes optimum performance on high speed ovals, such as the one in Indianapolis.

One necessary objective of equipment design and manufacturing is to manage (translation: limit) speed capability for the sake of maintaining safety while simultaneously reducing costs for the sake of vehicle affordability. There is a finite set of rules that maintain the integrity of the competition within the parameters of practical design and development constraints; options may be limited, deviations avoided, yet vehicle safety and consistency upheld. Today's IRL cars are produced in accordance with a set of standard regulations that CART, had it continued to exist, might also have implemented.

Chapter Twenty-Three

The phenomenal growth of The National Association of Stock Car Auto Racing (NASCAR) in the 1990's created more than an ephemeral challenge to the open-wheel racing sport in North America, which had formerly seen the Indianapolis 500 as the motor sports' only real focal priority. This sister sport sprouted and flourished at the same time open-wheel racing grappled with divisive politics within its own rival factions. Accomplished drivers, national celebrity, strong marketing, powerful media outlets, and attractive sponsorship came to serve, and continue today, as hallmark NASCAR characteristics.

Creating a clear identity for the CART series had been a challenge from inception. Lack of cohesive marketing within open-wheel racing likely served as one obstacle to its developing a solid following. Many people with little knowledge of auto-racing or this particular acronym, perceived CART racing to be KART (Go-Kart) racing. CART had leased use of the specific term *IndyCar* at the time of the organization's formation. Use of this might have provided a more distinct and readily recognizable identity, however, this option had not been pushed to the forefront of CART's branding effort. At the end of the day, the name Championship Auto Racing Teams (CART) had not seemed to foster the substantive nor lasting recognition it sought to achieve. Since the unification of open-wheel racing, the IRL has regained possession of that term and can now appropriately brand itself as *IndyCar* racing.

CHAPTER TWENTY-FOUR

Small, independent racing teams have long added interest to the Indy 500 for their one-off appearances at that event and within open-wheel racing overall. Financial factors have proven a primary challenge for them, however, often deterring them from running a full season. Over time, many teams have hung up their tools, downsized staff and either temporarily garaged or sold off cars as a result of being unable to sustain the high costs of racing. Vehicle and equipment expenses rise concurrently as the series level does. At the IndyCar level, these are the highest.

Some independent team owners value the technological freedom that non-standardized chassis and engine requirements permit. The ability to *build a better mousetrap* shifts some weight from driver capability to engineering know-how and ingenuity, which hearkens back to earlier days of race car development. Proponents of this position feel that free market competition amongst manufacturers will help keep costs reasonable. In particular, they may be less comfortable with what they perceive as the highly-escalated price of leasing sealed engines (in 2010, Honda) and/or purchasing the league's standardized specification chassis (in 2010, Dallara).

A differing school of thought attempts to level the playing field.

Standardizing the engine and chassis used intends to minimize quality differentials on these primary equipment expenditures. Standardization attempts to position driver skill as the influential performance factor. Still, arguments about the high costs of racing arise. Teams and drivers innovate with the equipment they have at their disposal, seeking to gain increased speeds down to fractions of seconds. Though strict guidelines exist regarding the assembly and use of much of their equipment, teams constantly tweak what they can in order to gain a competitive edge. With spending unregulated and some teams well-fortified with financial and technological resources, some are better-endowed than others, and can draw/sustain expensive, highly qualified engineers, mechanics and crew. These teams can research, test and tweak their equipment beyond that of what a number of other teams can afford to do. Whether specification or independently-designed vehicles are in use, wide variances in resource availability make it difficult to keep all things equal.

One small team owner, Paul Diatlovich of PDM Racing, is renowned and respected in the sport for functioning with low-budget operations. He has been a long-time participant on the open wheel racing car scene and in IndyCar racing since 1994. His shop is famous and historic. Diatlovich continues the tradition of one of the sport's most legendary builders and mechanics, A.J. Watson, who opened the first shop in Indy (late 1960s; this building now houses PDM Racing.) Stepping into Diatlovich's garage evokes an image of what might just be the most historic, fundamental and pure elements of race car preparation – no flash or frills – just a couple of guys with skill, passion, cars, and readiness to get their own hands dirty.

Diatlovich makes the most of those racing opportunities he can afford, yet rising costs have consistently been a challenge, and in his case, have recently become prohibitive. Fortunately, he has been able to fund his shop's continuation by providing cars and technicians for potential IndyCar drivers attempting to pass their rookie tests. Sixty drivers have obtained their

Chapter Twenty-Four

IRL competition licenses through his shop, including three-time IndyCar champion Sam Hornish, Jr., John Paul, Jr., Steve Knapp, Jimmy Kite, Jack Hewitt, Ed Carpenter, Billy Boat, Mark Dismore, and Eliseo Salazar.

Diatlovich had owned one of the three original IRL teams left in the IndyCar series, however in 2010, PDM has been priced out of regular competition at this level. Diatlovich has two Indy Lights vehicles in his shop and is competing in this still costly, but more affordable, second-tier series. Yet PDM longs to get back to full IndyCar representation.

Diatlovich doesn't believe that high-end operations should have to be necessary for producing strong car-and-driver combinations. As evidence, he points to the walls of his small Indianapolis shop, covered with photographs of those who have come through his operation. What is to be said about major operations being able to spend $10 million on drag reduction studies and adjustments when small shops up the road cannot afford to do so? Diatlovich shakes his head at the thought. He advocates cost-containment for IndyCar competitors, a spending cap. Where teams feel they cannot compete, they will be reluctant to participate. Where they cannot afford to do so, the decision will be made for them.

The answer is not simple. Exacting and maintaining the proper alchemy of chassis, engine, crew, driver and expense management to enforce the fairest and best of racing conditions is the sport's constant challenge.

CHAPTER TWENTY-FIVE

Early May 1998, a pick-up team of race team hopefuls turned up at the speedway with a used car and waited in pit lane for someone to pay attention to them. For two days, no one did. No Indy officials. No tire manufacturers. No one.

Then out of the blue, The Flying Hawaiian, Danny Ongais, walked up and asked new team owner Dale Pelfrey if he needed a driver. The answer was yes. They shook hands. Danny asked if Pelfrey would give him something if he won. *Of course!*

After the popular *Danny On-Gas* Ongais, eleven-time Indy-competitor, showed interest in the car, Indy people fell over themselves to help outfit him. Goodyear and Firestone reps offered tires. Helmut manufacturing provided Danny with helmets. Wow – what a difference! Danny didn't waste any time. With the help of engineering friends from competing teams, he set to work getting the car up to speed. Other participants didn't think this small team posed any serious challenge. They were wrong. In practice sessions, Pelfrey Car 81 went from the bottom of the speed charts to finishing in the top ten.

Shortly before qualification started, the right rear suspension broke entering Turn 2. Danny took 84 G's. He would recover, but the car was demolished from the rear wing to the fuel cell.

The crew went to work around-the-clock, borrowed an engine, gearbox, wing, etc. and rebuilt the car in time to be ready for the first day of qualifying. John Paul, Jr. asked to give the rebuilt race car a shakedown run. After running just two laps, he had to park the car. The engine Team Pelfrey possessed was showing low oil pressure. The team decided that John Paul, Jr. would try to get the four qualifying laps in before the engine blew. It was risky, but the gamble worked! He qualified 17th, middle of the grid.

With its only car in the race, Team Pelfrey's morale was great. The team (Dale Pelfrey, Don Basalla, Wayne Edwards, Ron Pelfrey, Rick Pelfrey, Terry Wilbert, Greg Paull, Richard Moyer, John Riser, Shawn Bayliff, Jason Gregg, Gary Gregg, Burt & Bernie Kearns) was able to get its engine back from rebuild and go through the car completely in preparation for the big event.

Race day came. The start for the first couple of laps was dicey. There were a couple of spins in Turn 1 on the first lap. Paul missed them, but just barely, and proceeded to move toward the front. He was heard to say that he could pass either high or low. About a quarter of the way into the race, he took the lead – the first time in his seven Indy 500's that he had led the race. He pulled ahead from the rest of the field and held his lead. The only exceptions to this were his taking pit stops under the green flag and one incident in which the yellow caution light in his cockpit lit up – a *slow down* warning. He slowed, yet others continued on. Paul soon discovered that his car appeared to be the only one receiving and responding to this signal. Finally, with 31 laps to go, Paul had made his last pit stop. He had still been holding a substantial lead, and would have rejoined the race in the first position, were it not for a broken shifter which hindered a timely re-start. His pit crew had to push/pull him back and forth four times before

Chapter Twenty-Five

the engine finally restarted and took hold. Had that late race problem not deterred him, it seems probable that Paul would have led 50 of the 200 laps and won the race. Instead he led 31 laps and finished seventh. This was still not a bad finish for Team Pelfrey's first race ever.

CHAPTER TWENTY-SIX

There was a plethora of open-wheel racing categories active in the United States in the mid-to-late 1990s, within which feasible IndyCar candidates might be discovered and developed. Tony George's declared intention of providing a path for American drivers to reach Indy had opened up opportunities which had not been available for many decades. No longer should it be necessary to spend thousands of dollars progressing through series upon series before reaching IndyCar-level racing. Now the door would be open for midget car racers and sprint car drivers, as well. As the Indy Racing League gained momentum, many of these drivers began to realize that the Indianapolis 500 lay within their grasp, and so, too, did many team owners who until now might never have given a serious thought to their dream of participating in the great race.

As it became clear that CART would not be joining the league and that most of the teams and drivers within that series would remain where they were, it also became increasingly evident that the early days of the IRL would then be primarily comprised of drivers with little to no experience at either an IndyCar level of competition or with this type of racecar. The organization was not without options. Lower-performance leagues had served as important resources for developing IndyCar driver capabilities; it was to these that the IRL now looked for its next crop of drivers to step up.

Simmering beneath the radar of most high-profile categories, Formula Ford 2000 was an established entry-level series in which many CART drivers and even Formula One drivers had first cut their teeth. Introduced in the 1970s, an FF2000 car was essentially a scaled-down IndyCar which included wings and slick tires. Running predominantly on a number of southern short-tracks, 150 mph FF2000 cars were putting on some spectacular races. This style of racing was in line with what the IRL needed to see from its drivers. As the handling characteristics of an FF2000 car were similar to those of an IndyCar, drivers were gaining unparalleled experience that prepared them for advancing into that higher echelon.

Driving midget and sprint cars, however, employed an entirely different driving technique. Making a direct transition from driving a midget or sprint car into a 200+ mph IndyCar might have been asking for a close encounter with the wall.

There seemed to have been several safety aspects of George's new series that would require attention. The most fundamental problem, however, would remain the somewhat obscure identities of that cast of drivers who would compete in the first year of the series – specifically, the 33 drivers who were projected to sit on the starting grid of the 1996 Indianapolis 500 – if, indeed, a total of 33 qualified drivers could be rallied. The skeptics had their doubts. The reputation of the Indy 500 usually did draw an array of drivers, many of whom had established reputations already at the speedway, but George was just as ready to pluck his drivers from obscurity. As 1996 progressed and teams prepared for the opening round at the new Walt Disney World Speedway in Orlando, fans were eager to see who the stars of this year's big show would be. In the absence of such luminaries as Roger Penske, Carl Haas, Paul Newman, Pat Patrick and Gerry Forsythe, team owners who

Chapter Twenty-Six

had, in some cases, carried IndyCar Racing for more than a decade, the IRL pitched its tent in Florida for the start of a season that was highly uncertain and bore more questions than answers. How would this new league be received? How many teams would show up? And importantly, how many fans would walk through the gates?

The 1996 season saw drivers emerge from all racing disciplines. They came from Indy Lights, the established feeder series for CART. There were ex-Formula One drivers, a smattering of foreign drivers with fading reputations in their home countries, soon-to-be-graduates from Formula Ford 2000 racing, and an array of midget and sprint car drivers, primarily from the Midwest. Oh, and did stock car drivers get a mention? Some had multiple years of experience and were performing at the apex of their careers. Some were former champions, others journeymen drivers, still others professionals at driving *just about anything with a steering wheel.* There were names with no labels, hopefuls who had just enough experience in something to legitimately participate in the event.

This was a brave new world and George was now master of his own domain. But at what cost? Sponsors were not flocking to his door. Nor, it seemed, were they eager to get on with the fledgling teams. It was clear that his muscle was the Indianapolis Motor Speedway and the Indianapolis 500. Names on both sides of the transporters were predominantly proprietary – there were no big sponsors involved – just the names of team owners themselves, generally those with middling income who saw this as their opportunity to finally get into the big race. That first year might have provided the impression that IndyCar racing had thrown open its doors to glorified amateurs.

In a way, it had. The Indy Racing League had never intended to emulate CART. It sought to be an entirely new series, composed of the most fundamental aspects of open-wheel racing with a slant toward reduced costs, simplified technology, greater inclusiveness of participants at the grassroots level and heightened encouragement of involvement by American drivers and teams.

CHAPTER TWENTY-SEVEN

Walking around the garage area at the Indianapolis Motor Speedway is much like being backstage at a theater before the performance begins. Unlike the theater, however, the public has full access to these "dressing rooms." Gasoline Alley casts a spell over those who enter. Garage doors are opened for gawking viewers to pause over the awe-inspiring engineering masterpieces resting within. Even disassembled, these objects look impressive, and spectators gaze, transfixed by each remote component or stroke of mechanical finesse. A racecar is a thing of beauty. Whether at rest, elevated, still, humming, or poised to lunge down the track, it attracts admiration.

On a pre-race night, while Indianapolis sleeps, the world within the speedway is yet dynamic and bustling; many teams work through the darkness to prepare their cars for the next day's activities. Though not the predetermined plan, sleepless nights are a regular expectation for most racing mechanics. There always seems to be one more task that must be done and at least a dozen other activities which must precede it. Often cars arrive to the mechanics in pieces, perhaps coming straight from previous races, where damage was incurred. A racecar is designed to function as a whole, yet it is the sum of parts functioning individually and collectively which dictate optimum performance. Each part will be checked, tweaked, rechecked, and checked yet again.

The delicate procedure of *setting up* a racecar is a study in patience and precision. The chassis, the *shell* of the car in which the driver sits, is the backbone of the car. This is attached to the engine, gearbox, suspension and wheels. Chassis set-up involves careful attentiveness to wheel alignment, spring, shock- and ride-height adjustment, brake balance and suspension. Each of these is significant in achieving maximum performance, and a driver's best use of these, even within a standardized vehicle, may be significant in seeking his edge over other competitors.

All of this must work in unison. Any of these components could result in dysfunction if not appropriately considered, tweaked and locked into place. One wrong adjustment could cancel out all others. The impact of each specific setting could mean the difference of nearly one mile per hour, which at Indy, could make the difference between a car's qualifying to race or not.

Aerodynamics play a predominant role in how well a car functions; front and rear wings together with an array of *winglets*, attached to the chassis must all be set at complementary angles. These serve the flow of air over the car and provide the *downforce* needed to give the tires optimum grip, and often to stop the car from literally lifting off, becoming airborne. Gear ratio match to the engine torque determine the optimum performance needed to pull a car through the corners and down the straights. Other considerations affecting aerodynamics include wind direction, wind speed, tread and ambient temperatures, etc.

Experienced teams and drivers arrive with considerable car performance data gathered from past races. They use this as a starting point from which to work. Telemetry modules set up in pits monitor car performance on the

Chapter Twenty-Seven

track and feed back such recorded information as revs per minute, throttle and brake application, steering input, suspension loads, g-forces and tire pressures. This data is transmitted to analysts and engineers, who interpret readouts and provide directions to either the driver on the track (cockpit tweaks) or to nearby mechanics (pit adjustments).

To maximize car performance, a driver must juggle a variety of critical functions simultaneously while on the track. He thinks about vehicle information provided to him by his crew chief and in return, monitors and relays feedback about the car's handling. He has his hands full simply maintaining control over the often unwieldy, unpredictable beast that is his car, seeking to direct it along the best driving lines at the quickest speeds without losing imperative tire traction with the asphalt surface.

In addition to these functions, there is the voice in his headset monitoring ever-shifting raceway and traffic conditions, advising as to the advantages, warnings and limitations within his grasp at any given moment. Individuals posted atop the highest locations around the track, usually on the roof of the grandstand, follow the cars as they circulate at speed, maintain radio contact with drivers, and advise them on track conditions and race circumstances that could impact both their position and safety. A *spotter* is a driver's extra pair of eyes, watching ahead of and around a car as it negotiates each lap. A spotter addresses everything from incidents on the track, cars behind or alongside, shifting weather conditions and the progress or fallback of nearby competitors. From the first use of radio communications within cars to today, the spotter's job has become increasingly important; a driver relies more and more implicitly upon the guidance he is given. Split-second analysis communicated by an experienced spotter to a quickly-responding driver can make the difference between a car's gaining or losing several positions on a single lap.

With so much critical input affecting track performance, mechanics must ensure that their car is tight and ready to go. While a driver sleeps, mechanics burn the midnight oil to prepare their machines for the following day's challenges, basing their specificity of adjustments and final set-up upon the predetermined goal of each session. Is the driver going for speed this time? Is he working to improve vehicle handling? To improve fuel economy? Or is the specific challenge or problem one that has not yet been identified or defined? Mechanics work through a checklist of possible adjustments in pursuit of the best possible vehicle performance.

CHAPTER TWENTY-EIGHT

Drivers must maintain a high degree of physical fitness and mental conditioning. The *Sunday drive*, for them, is anything but a leisurely jaunt. Circulating a racecar at speeds approaching 240 mph over periods of two to three hours (sometimes four to five) can drain drivers' strength. So intense are the physical and mental demands, that some have been known to lose several pounds of weight during the course of a single race. Sharp concentration is paramount to both success and survival. Simultaneously maintaining awareness of what is happening around them on all sides, processing the data displayed, adjusting for shifting conditions, responding to radio guidance given and paying attention to the movements of other cars – all within fractions of seconds – these are critical priorities. Gravitational force (g-force) consistently pulling upon head, neck and shoulder muscles with each turn of the steering wheel and every push of the throttle takes its toll.

Speeds through each of Indy's four turns are in excess of 200 mph. On a fast lap, a driver will neither brake nor remove his foot from the gas. As cars move through each corner, forces working on both car and driver will sufficiently slow a vehicle, enabling it to progress through the turn on the projected line, often skimming the wall as it exits. Speed will be *scrubbed*, frictional forces working on the tires and lateral g-forces working against the car, slow it to around 200 mph in the turns. Average lap speeds at this time are expected to come in around 220 mph. Totaling the laps a driver might accomplish within practice and racing equates one strenuous workout!

CHAPTER TWENTY-NINE

The opening of the speedway for the 2009 activities marked the official beginning of the Indianapolis Motor Speedway Centennial Era 2009-2011, commemorating one-hundred years since Carl Fisher and his partners formally opened the track in 1909 and the inaugural 500 mile race two years later.

Attempting to qualify for the first time were six rookie drivers who had never before raced in the Indy 500. It is tough enough for experienced drivers to come and contend with all of the implications of this venue and race. Even the most grizzled of veterans will tell you that driving here can be the most gut-wrenching challenge a driver will endure.

So for Mike Conway, Stanton Barrett, Nelson Philippe, Raphael Matos, Robert Doornbos and the new driver for Conquest Racing, Alex Tagliani, one can only imagine the knots in their stomachs as they prepared for their obligatory rookie orientation. As all of them were experienced professional racing drivers, some with exceptional achievements, the term *rookie* could seem misleading. But until they had raced the Indy 500, that is what they were considered here.

From all corners of the globe, they knew what Indy represented. Many were following in the footsteps of their own countrymen who had themselves achieved great success here. Brazilians Emerson Fittipaldi and Helio Castroneves, French-Canadian Jacques Villeneuve, British drivers Jim Clark, Graham Hill, Dan Wheldon and Dario Franchitti, as well as Dutchman Arie Luyendyk, were all international winners of this great race who had had their images cast upon the Borg-Warner trophy. Along with rookie contemporaries who had yet to make their mark, Wheldon, Franchitti and Castroneves were eager to taste the winner's milk in Victory Lane once more.

Just as each had come from a different racing background, each had, in his own way, learned to manage the pressures of life in the fast lane. When one has built his life around the pursuit of speed, when he has groomed his identity around being a racecar driver, he has probably also learned to disguise the nerves and inherent fears that go hand-in-hand with the occupation.

Fear is something that few drivers will admit to having. Some will rarely confess to being frightened, others believe that fear should be openly acknowledged, even welcomed. Some of the greatest drivers have declared themselves to hold a healthy propensity toward fear, contending that as a critical warning system, it is the one emotion that might actually save their lives. They see it as something to be recognized and respected. Successful racecar drivers continue to be cognizant of dangerous situations, recognize their own limitations and avoid foolhardy risk-taking which could ultimately cost them their lives.

There is a certain ambivalent approach to handling Indy that many drivers experience when they arrive at the speedway for the first time. They instruct themselves to treat it as they would any other track. "*Don't be intimidated by it. Just do what you have always done – drive.*" Still, this is Indy. How does one get that out of his head?

A rookie must put aside all distractions and concentrate solely upon the task

Chapter Twenty-Nine

of completing a set number of laps at progressively increasing speeds under the watchful eyes of race officials who will assess his capability of driving at competition level.

As the curtain went up on Act I, Scene I of the 2009 Indianapolis 500, there was anticipation in the air and adrenaline in the veins. Gasoline Alley was alive with activity as the garages opened for business. Engineers and mechanics made final preparations to cars before they took to the track for their first laps.

The first two days on Indianapolis' raceway are reserved for rookies and those needing to re-acclimatize themselves to the course – drivers who have raced it before, but have not driven it in some time. Among those names in 2009 were Paul Tracy, Scott Sharp, Alex Lloyd, A.J. Foyt, IV, Davey Hamilton, John Andretti, and former winner Buddy Lazier. Their hitting the track along with the first-timers made for some busy sessions.

An ear-piercing scream shattered the silence as the first engine fired up. Then another and another. The ritual of parading the cars from the garages through Gasoline Alley to the pits was underway. We saw for the first time the brightly-gleaming colors and distinctive logos of that year's contenders. Those teams who qualified would live in Gasoline Alley for nearly three weeks. Everyone here would get to know the faces in these familiar places. They would rub shoulders with friends and strangers alike. Though there were many garages, everyone here would be under the same roof. For 28 days, they would share each other's gain and pain.

The shrieking tones of Honda V-8 engines reverberated through Gasoline Alley. Rookies hoping to wear the mantle of speedway drivers were to now prove their capability of driving with the best. Many would draw on the advice and experience of drivers who had gone before, in some cases, previous champions like Johnny Rutherford, Rick Mears, Arie Luyendyk, and Al and Bobby Unser, who now acted as formal advisors or consultants to both drivers and teams. Others relied upon the experience of team owners and crew chiefs who possessed abundant knowledge and discernment. Having the perspective and input of these seasoned veterans was invaluable.

After studies and briefings, drivers were soon alone in their cockpits, helmets on, visors down, ready to go. The light turned green, the drama began. Drivers selected first gear, increased their revs and slowly moved forward onto the speedway track.

After three or four laps each returned to the pits for a *systems check* – to make sure that there were no leaks, that nothing had worked loose, that everything was still functioning as intended. Drivers returned again to the track for some exploratory laps, picking up speed as they felt their cars settle into steady rhythm. They worked to build relationships with both car and track. Not too fast at first. They invested critical effort into gaining a feel for the strengths, challenges and intricacies of each. Moving slowly and with precision, they tested their vehicles' interplay with the track surface, slope and external conditions. As understanding kicked in, patterns were discerned, equipment tweaked, problems spotted and resolved, speed followed. Confidence increased over successive laps until drivers reached that zenith at which their apprehensions dissipated and they felt certain they were ready to race.

For newcomers especially, this *getting-to-know-you* session served both driver and support team together. They attempted to complete as many laps as they could – often, just as many as they could afford – all the while carefully studying the car and making adjustments in search of optimal performance.

Now in the spotlight, some for the first time here, unchoreographed, but not unprepared, drivers found their footing. Passing the rookie test is a rite of passage initiating a driver into the privilege of racing the Indy 500. This had been the first important stepping stone leading up to the big day. These 2009 rookies were then able to turn attention to the next big challenge of meeting race qualification requirements.

CHAPTER THIRTY

The IMS Security Patrol, affectionately dubbed *Yellow Shirts*, is ostensibly the mechanism that permits the speedway to organize its functions effectively. These volunteers support the multiple working parts that revolve around the demands of visitors and spectators for such an event as the Indy 500.

Yellow Shirts abound at the Indianapolis Motor Speedway like bees buzzing around a hive. These revered marshals are in place to guide, inform, advise, enlighten, illuminate, instruct, and often demand, command, or reprimand. They man the gates, parking lots, stands and suites. Overseeing Gasoline Alley, the garages and the pits, they keep traffic flowing and people moving. They are not only the eyes and ears of the speedway's management, but also provide the essential services that support speedway event activities throughout the month of May. Situated on the ninth floor of the Pagoda Tower, overlooking the Start/Finish straightaway, are the offices of the organizations and agencies assigned the responsibilities of public safety and security. Some coordinate police, fire and medical services. Others serve as homeland security, FBI and Secret Service agents or serve in the Federal Aviation Administration. Yellow Shirts are the speedway's lieutenants on the ground, often the first respondents to an emergency or crisis situation involving spectators, employees or track officials.

They view themselves and each other as a family, many returning each May to their same posts and responsibilities at the track. There are some 1,800 Yellow Shirts in attendance on race day, like a small army, keeping order and ensuring that everyone is in the proper place. Visitors to the speedway find them to be helpful, friendly, efficient and hospitable.

CHAPTER THIRTY-ONE

Though for many teams and drivers the oval configuration of the Indianapolis Motor Speedway track is familiar, the protocol standard and the schedule part of their regular season, no one regards the Indy 500 as *just another race*. The whole preceding month is an event, a happening. Off-track, drivers and high profile team members contend with multiple appointments and social obligations – sponsor functions, community events, media appearances and interviews – which begin upon arrival. Drivers barely have time to unpack suitcases and shower before the barrage of requests is underway.

A culture valuing celebrity and behind-the-scenes glimpses of impending events can place excessive demands upon a driver's time. It seems that everyone wants access to him – the bigger his name – the more requests for access. We talk of a driver who, years ago, would race two, perhaps three times a week in different racing disciplines, arriving in Indianapolis from a small or obscure track elsewhere because driving served as his fulltime vocation. Today, drivers sustain full calendars for other reasons. Many jet from one appearance to another to satisfy sometimes demanding expectations of sponsors, media and fans. The unfolding schedule in Indianapolis continues and most likely escalates these ongoing obligations. It is all part of being a star on this particular stage.

Top drivers often have managers who take care of the business/media end of their responsibilities, freeing drivers to focus their efforts upon the more performance-based aspects of the profession. Unfortunately, in some cases, this has led to drivers making fewer personal connections with their fan base and the media – less than ideal for pleasing sponsors or cultivating loyal supporters. This challenge is by no means exclusive to motor sports. Permitting celebrities to segregate performance and social tasks has inadvertently stretched a broader divide between themselves and those who demand access to them.

When not on the track or consulting with engineers, drivers often pass the time in their motor homes. In the garage area, fans are quick to notice popular figures. On more informal days, stars are more accessible and approachable for attentively signing autographs or patiently posing for photos. Some embrace the crowds warmly and converse with them as if they were old friends. Others may be more standoffish, showing less interest in interaction. However, auto racing prides itself on the accessibility of its drivers. Sponsors and the IRL approve of this practice and encourage it amongst its teams.

Are there limitations as to what constitutes reasonable, feasible access, even to the most welcoming of professionals? Often inundated with requests for interviews, personal appearances, photo and autograph sessions, drivers work to balance social responsibilities with the already demanding challenges of race preparation and driving. Many drivers utilize public relations professionals to help them compartmentalize their daily routine and prioritize activities.

Each driver has his own process for securing the mental focus he will take onto the track – some popular warm-up activities include relaxing,

Chapter Thirty-One

reading, meditating, listening to music, or playing computer games. Working around a defined track schedule, a driver's non-race day at the track might begin with a short run and light breakfast, then a session in the gym with a personal trainer, followed by meetings with team personnel and engineers to discuss any new developments. Meetings with sponsors and media, as well as promotional appearances at local venues, will be scheduled around on-track activities – or better yet, arranged for days when the raceway lies quiet.

As the big show begins, one's role is defined. Each person may participate, but will he be a valued, solicited contender? Will he achieve special status, notoriety amongst his peers? For newcomers and those who have not raced regularly in some time, current performance capability is a legitimate question mark and a frequent topic of speculation. Sometimes there are surprises where one would expect greater clarity and confidence. Even established drivers with winning reputations and records of strong recent achievements approach this landmark event with greater uncertainty than self-assurance. Indianapolis can be unpredictable. Those who have participated in the Indy 500 know better than to take anything for granted, such as to presume he will qualify for a race because he has been successful at other venues or because he has been racing well recently. Indeed, it all comes down to the moment – those particular inputs and circumstances on that given day. Just ask respected team owner Roger Penske, whose team was favored to excel in 1995. That year, neither of the two cars his team entered for the race successfully qualified, despite the fact that both drivers, Emerson Fittipaldi and Al Unser, Jr., had already won the Indy 500 multiple times. It is fair to say that going into the month of May, everyone feels that he has a chance at qualifying, even winning. At this place, anything can happen – and often does. As suitcases are unpacked, garages equipped, motor homes parked, cars roll off trailers and crews prepare, there is a sense of excitement, spirit of camaraderie, feeling of belonging. All anticipate the event. No one has been eliminated. It lies within each team's grasp. It's as if the whole racing world is together in this place, all people familiar faces – friends. Each person has his part to play and in Indianapolis is exactly where he wants to be.

CHAPTER THIRTY-TWO

For three or four weeks every May, Indianapolis becomes, among other things, the social capital of America's sporting world. During that period, there are collectively more gatherings, fund-raising events, corporate functions, celebrity bashes and parties than one might find in New York and Los Angeles combined. Appearances by team drivers, sponsor promotions, golf tournaments and fashion shows abound, culminating with the Indy 500 Festival Parade the week of the race. There is plenty to occupy residents, guests and racing interests as the month progresses.

Philanthropy has always played a significant role in the festivities. Thousands of dollars are raised for local charities each year, with many groups and causes benefiting directly from contributions made by the racing community, businesses and general public. The Hulman family has been a dedicated contributor for a number of years to such esteemed Indiana establishments as Indiana State University and their local Terre Haute Rose Polytechnic Institute, now the Rose-Hulman Institute of Technology. Each year, new creative activities spring up across the city, from themed *milk-chugging* contests to ping-pong tournaments, drawing the attendance and dollars of those interested in participating in the latest causes and pastimes.

For drivers and sports personalities, these equate to photo opportunities, soirees at which to mingle, a chance to rub shoulders with an abundance of colleagues, friends and personalities courting celebrity.

Many fundraisers are breathing a sigh of relief at the revived abundance of this year's activities. Following the split, there had been a severe decline in revenue collected, with some activities even being cancelled for lack of involvement. Yet as star names have begun returning to the speedway, so too have the participants of previously curtailed events. The 2008 Indy 500, the first after unification, saw a significant increase in contributions, and this past year (2009) witnessed a flurry of activity as many organizations regrouped to capitalize upon the new era in open wheel racing. In spite of continued economic challenges, optimism abounds.

The motor sporting community has generally been quick to come to the aid of those in need. From drivers and team owners to sponsors and fans, there has rarely been a shortage of support for a worthy cause. Many competitors have been personally touched by circumstances deeply affecting their own lives, and have found that their own celebrity has provided them an uncommon benefit – a platform for promoting those causes which move them. They influence others to share in philanthropic matters, as well.

One of these organizations includes the Sam Schmidt Paralysis Foundation, founded by Sam Schmidt, a former IndyCar driver in three Indy 500 races, before he was injured in a testing crash at the Walt Disney World Speedway in 2000. Schmidt is now a quadriplegic who participates in benevolent activities and owns a team racing in Indy Lights, the driver development series for aspiring IndyCar drivers. Sam Schmidt Motorsports is the all-time victory leader in the Indy Lights championship with 30 race wins and three driver titles and has qualified nine entries in the Indy 500 since 2001. Sam Schmidt Motorsports teamed with Chris Ganassi Racing in 2009 to enter driver Alex Lloyd in the Indy 500. Lloyd finished in 13th place. The combined teams will again enter a car in the 2010 Indy 500.

Chapter Thirty-Two

Target Team Chip Ganassi maintains an ongoing relationship with St. Jude Children's Research Hospital, and donates fixed sums based upon race results, laps completed, etc. Its involvement, together with that of Ganassi sponsor Target, continues to help raise the profile of the hospital and spread the message of hope to hundreds of children afflicted with cancer and other life-threatening illnesses.

Another organization is inspired by Cody Unser, daughter of former Indy500 winner Al Unser, Jr., and granddaughter of four-time Indy 500 winner Al Unser, Sr. Cody woke up one morning to discover that she couldn't walk. A victim of the spinal cord disease *transverse myelitus*, she has been confined to a wheelchair since the age of 12. With her mother Shelley, she has established the Cody Unser First Step Foundation to raise money for research into spinal cord-related paralysis and continues to offer hope to other victims through her personal appearances and speeches. Cody was inspired by the late Christopher Reeve and continues the quest begun by the courageous movie star.

Major fundraisers are held for multiple other charities, including Riley Children's Hospital in Indianapolis, the Lyn St. James Foundation and Disabled American Veterans (DAV).

CHAPTER THIRTY-THREE

Sarah Fisher eased herself into the cockpit of her Dallara-Honda and geared up for the 2009 Indianapolis 500. Her fears were not based upon personal injury, lack of confidence, nor intimidation; Sarah's concerns were centered upon money, or rather, the shortage of it. Sarah has been one of the most tenacious drivers competing at the speedway. One of three women entered for the race, along with Danica Patrick and Milka Duno, it was Sarah who set the early standard for female drivers in the Indy Racing League.

In keeping with Tony George's early goal of helping American drivers participate in IndyCar racing, in particular those grassroots aspirants in USAC sprint and midget car racing, IRL team owner Dale Pelfrey picked up the phone in 1999 and offered Sarah a drive in his car. At the age of 18, Sarah became the youngest driver to pass the rookie test to become a full IndyCar racer. Sarah raced only once with Team Pelfrey, but having achieved this early visibility and experience, she was on her way up.

Sarah's IRL series debut came in 1999 at the Texas Motor Speedway where she raced for Team Pelfrey. In 2000, she ran eight IndyCar series races with the Walker Racing team. She became the youngest person to lead an IndyCar race and the youngest woman to finish in a podium position, a third place finish at Kentucky Motor Speedway. In May 2000, she became the third woman and one of the youngest drivers to ever compete in the Indy 500. Though she had managed to secure a number of sponsors throughout her race year, she achieved only enough funding to race a limited program. Her overall result in the championship perhaps did not provide an accurate reflection of her full potential.

In 2001, again driving for Derrick Walker, she completed a full racing season. Highlights included her finishing an IRL series race at Miami-Homestead Speedway in second place – the best IndyCar series achievement by a woman up to this point. At the end of the season, she was voted IndyCar series' *Most Popular Driver*, a distinction she would be awarded in 2002 and 2003, as well.

In 2002, in spite of missing several races for lack of sponsorship, she again achieved distinction at Kentucky Motor Speedway, becoming the first woman to win a pole position. She then went on to lead the first 26 laps of that race.

But success has not come easily for Sarah. Plucky and undaunted, she continued racing for the next several years, both in the IRL and in a number of NASCAR races on the west coast. As Danica Patrick's star began to shine, so it was that Sarah's may have lost some twinkle. It almost seemed as if the media could focus on only one woman driver at a time and Danica, new on the scene, had captured their attention. Whereas Danica embraced her publicity, Sarah had quietly, resolutely continued her pursuit of driving IndyCars.

At the end of 2007, after driving an unremarkable season for Dreyer & Reinbolt Racing, she began hatching plans to start her own team. It would be an ambitious move, but one that could certainly be rewarding if she

Chapter Thirty-Three

proved successful. She announced her intentions of competing in the 2008 Indy 500 under Sarah Fisher Racing. Scraping together enough funding to purchase the needed equipment, which included mortgaging her house, she arrived at the Indianapolis Motor Speedway as an owner/driver for her seventh attempt at establishing a new record. This was her most ambitious to date – that of being the first woman to win the Indy 500.

But 2008 was to be no fairy tale for Sarah. Her Indy 500 race ended when Tony Kanaan spun in front of her and both cars hit the wall. Sarah surveyed her severely damaged car and the emotion seemed overwhelming. Having borrowed, begged and worked tirelessly to assemble a new team, with long days and nights preparing for this day, she now saw her opportunity and investment hanging from the hook of a tow truck. Adding insult to injury, a sponsor had failed to make a promised payment at a critical time. Sarah's introduction into IndyCar team ownership had been a painful one, but she did not give up. Less than two months later, she secured the backing of Dollar General and was able to score a couple more races before ending that season with a second wall encounter at Chicagoland Speedway.

Tenacity and resourcefulness have pulled her through. Sarah has proven time and time again that she is a worthy contender in competition. Almost 10 years since those first tentative laps behind the wheel of Dale Pelfrey's IndyCar, her career has seen highs and lows that would have deterred many male contenders. Sarah commands the dignity and respect of her contemporaries.

Now in the dual roles of racecar driver and team owner, Sarah bears diverse responsibilities. Sometimes when a team's driver also serves as its owner, the running memory of his bank account total can hinder willingness to take risks and be as forceful on the track as is needed. One incident, as Sarah knows all too well, could send her home. She cannot let such thoughts interfere with the drive, however. Sustaining the right balance of priorities is critical.

In 2010, Sarah's focus is on building a competitive team. She continues to retain the support of Dollar General, and now Direct Supply, as well as a small group of contingency sponsors.

Shortly before the inaugural race of the 2010 IndyCar season in St. Petersburg, FL, Sarah made a generous move – she hired skilled driver Graham Rahal and started him in the first race, relinquishing her own spot in order to seat a team member who had recently been driving faster on road courses than she had. It was a move she believed would better favor the team's overall success. Rahal finished in ninth place after running as high as third or fourth at times. The team continues to work out its strategy, plans to soon add an additional car and will progress to running full season schedules. The near-term goal is to aim for consistent finishes within in the top ten. Onlookers watch their progress with interest.

CHAPTER THIRTY-FOUR

In March 2010, Roger Bailey, Executive Director of Firestone Indy Lights and Tony George Jr., Manager of Business Development for Firestone Indy Lights, introduced a new, formalized driver development ladder, *The Road to Indy*, designed to provide a comprehensive tiered program for aspiring IndyCar drivers.

Uniting diversified efforts into a single cohesive program, getting all series pulling in the same direction, spending resources in the same areas and using consistent rulebooks is designed to streamline requirements, help minimize confusion and propel forward momentum for drivers moving upward through the series. Another positive aspect is that on scheduled professional weekends, *The Road to Indy* program unites various individual series into a multi-race event at the same venue on a given weekend, thereby maximizing visibility and experience for sponsors, teams and drivers at all levels.

From a driver's perspective, having a defined ladder and clear expectations eases his or her transition to faster, more demanding cars. It reduces anxiety about making sure he is developing the skills he most needs and eases questions he may have about whether he is spending valuable financial resources in the most appropriate manner.

Team owners and coaches should appreciate that adherence to a single, defined, tiered program will help avoid gaps in driver knowledge, experience or comfort level. Each tier provides street and road course track time. Drivers learn about varied surfaces and barriers and grow accustomed to increasingly complex levels of telemetry (data acquisition about vehicle performance useful in helping engineers set proper car parameters).

The first level is the USF2000. Drivers progress from there into The Star Mazda series and then into Indy Lights before moving to a full IndyCar level. Each series increases in vehicle construction, complexity, handling ability and horsepower.

As a formalized process, The Road to Indy ladder is still new, yet for the most part involves an alignment of established programs and resources rather than a reinvention of them. Indy Lights and Star Mazda are already well-populated and underway. With the USF2000 being newly reintroduced in 2010, herein probably lies the greatest opportunity for growth.

What skills does a contemporary driver need the most? The answer might be surprising. Bailey, George, and developing drivers agree that increasingly the most critical characteristic today's driver requires is the ability to raise capital via sponsorships. Driving capability surely counts, and may compose up to fifty percent of the ratio, yet the financial component of this ratio is more significant than ever. Rising costs of racing teamed with economic recession and the trend of corporate sponsorships going to top drivers often leaves the rest of the field, especially those not backed by strong family fortunes, struggling for sufficient finances to cover their rides. Drivers who were once traditionally supported by families, friends and small businesses, frequently now come up short. A driver who can raise $500,000 seed money to go racing is one who will merit a serious look from team owners.

Chapter Thirty-Four

Drivers striving to maintain and further their rides now turn as much attention to off-track marketing (public image, presentation, branding, calculating and promoting a probable return on investment for potential sponsors). Maintaining sponsorship continues to be a challenge for teams and drivers, especially those with larger corporate financiers who may be less likely to have personal interaction with the people representing their investments. Larger organizations stand a more probable chance than smaller ones of internally shifting assignments or having endorsement decisions determined by external forces who may have little interest in or knowledge of auto racing. Impact upon the corporate bottom line often plays a greater determining factor here than it does in smaller organizations, where softer, more subjective factors, such as personal relationships, uniting team behind a common cause, favorite driver, etc. figure more prominently.

CHAPTER THIRTY-FIVE

Twenty-year-old driver Shannon McIntosh is looking for her ride. Not content to sit back and await discovery, this racecar driver places continual thought into the strategy and marketing of her brand and asserts it every day in pursuit of her career.

Raised in a family with no auto-racing culture or experience and few discretionary funds to spend on driver development, Shannon has commenced down her career track with few of the natural advantages that have provided a leg up for several contemporaries; she has had to work hard to align her own stars. From an early age, she has recognized the value of promoting her own brand and has expected that she would have to be strategic and creative about getting in front of the right people to sell them on her capability.

She studies marketing, hones her interpersonal skills and picks up the phone with confidence to ask for what she needs. Attuned to the business side of racing, she seeks to discern and fulfill team and sponsor interests. Away from the track, she applies her branding skills in the sports marketing field, which regularly steeps her in the concepts of developing strong image and solid value proposition.

An early adopter of social media, Shannon utilizes such tools as Facebook and e-newsletters to nurture and expand her fan base. Frequent updates on events and notes of interest keep Shannon's brand in front of those following her career. She sums up her personal drive, persistence, presence and appreciation for support received as *gracious tenacity*.

Confident, polished, and determined, Shannon often studies on her own time and travels on her own dime to advance her driving career. She understands the value of maximizing whatever situation she is in and of being in the right place at the right moment. She travels cross-country to attend events and build and nurture her own network of professional relationships. She participates in charitable functions and rolls up her sleeves to work alongside teams hosting their own sponsors. Pulling up stakes from her hometown of Dayton, OH, she has recently moved to Indianapolis to immerse herself in the sport, culture, people and opportunities she hopes will positively influence her career.

At ease moving her way up from the back of the field, Shannon enjoys accomplishment achieved through striving. Her experience primarily lies in racing dirt and asphalt oval tracks in midget cars, though she has made recent forays into road racing, as well. While a winner of several regional and track races, financial limitations have not yet permitted her to drive for a full season. Frustrated about not yet securing the financing she needs, but eager to get back behind the wheel of a car, Shannon is ready to learn and committed to doing the work.

One such driver has achieved a leg up. Nick Andries, a quiet, persistent 19-year old from Pinellas Park, FL has secured a multi-year contract racing for Team Pelfrey in a national series for 2010 and beyond. He is working hard to hone his skills and develop a solid driving resume. His family has pulled out all the stops in scraping together the resources needed for him to go racing, and his mother has accompanied him at races and on the road, serving as coach, manager, marketer and cheerleader in bringing him this

Chapter Thirty-Five

far. Family and friends have been supportive, yet even so, outside assistance has been necessary to provide Andries' career with racing continuity over the years.

Never has that been more important than it is this season. Having caught the eye years ago of a former team owner who started early and continues to sponsor his development, Andries is now on the radar of those coaches, experienced racers and industry principals who have encountered him; they watch his career with interest. Of young drivers, Andries is particularly valued for his studious habits, discipline, and role model strength. Importantly, he can deliver wins.

Taking nothing for granted, Andries is a serious student of racecraft who cultivates proper driving technique and discipline. His background involved 13 years of karting before he entered and distinguished himself last year within the Skip Barber regional series. In his first year with that program, he won 11 out of 14 races, took a second and two thirds in the remaining ones, and secured the combined Midwest and Eastern Skip Barber regional championship (*Summer Series*). Such accomplishment has earned him the respect of his peers.

Andries analyzes courses, videotapes his drives and spends evenings before races and between on-track sessions sequestered in his hotel room scrutinizing these, discerning how to best maximize his performance. He attends seminars, asks good questions, takes notes and diligently applies the guidance and feedback he receives from coaches and engineers. His early performance record speaks for his achievement.

Off the track, Andries cultivates supplemental skills to enhance the breadth and depth of his knowledge. Up to this point, he has been responsible for his own car adjustments. Now a college student majoring in mechanical engineering, he believes this will help him better understand and respond to the fine-tuning of his cars. Researching and recommending program and race options for his team owner strengthens his capability on the business side of racing, as well.

Notably, both young drivers are fiercely committed, modest, sincere, hardworking and pay their dues. The one with financial backing will gain valuable seed time, experience and finesse his craft. The one without still seeks her moment to shine.

CHAPTER THIRTY-SIX

The great pre-war Grand Prix driver Achille Varzi reputedly believed that when he was on the racetrack, he was being chased by the devil. Once, when asked how he could string together an inordinate amount of exceptionally fast laps, the late Gilles Villeneuve replied simply, "I only look forward. I don't look back."* His 1995 Indy 500 winning son, Jacques, is on record as saying that he thought that racecars should not have mirrors. It would be more entertaining for everyone if drivers just focused on what was ahead and let those who were behind do just the same. It would make overtaking that much more, well, exciting. Yes, it is important to know what is behind and alongside, but most importantly, a driver needs to concentrate upon what lies ahead. Good drivers, it is said, use more than their eyes to see. They can sense what is around them. They can feel unrelenting pursuers pressing closer and can smell those within their grasp. Whatever a driver's position, his goal is to stay ahead of those behind and pass all those in front of him.

The notion of Varzi's devil may seem extreme to some, but this illusion served to effectively motivate him. Driving a racecar demands a certain state of mind. In professional parlance, this is often regarded as being *in the zone* – the ultimate psychological condition which reflects an ability to remove all competing thoughts from one's mind other than those needed for completing the task at hand. Drivers wrestle to curtail extraneous thoughts and unwelcome interruptions. Those unfamiliar with an athlete's need for streamlining his focus in preparation for a major feat or event may unwittingly step in his path or speak out of turn, resulting in unpleasant consequences. In those moments, the athlete may be perceived as aloof, disingenuous or arrogant. Offense may be given or taken.

While drivers contend with pressure differently, the fundamental dangers inherent in life behind the wheel, predicate an overt sense of being able to focus on the moment. A driver begins preparing mentally for his race, practice laps, or qualifying run for days leading up to these events. Some respond by placing communicative distance between themselves and those nonessential to the task at hand. Others use relaxation or visualization techniques, positive thinking, meditation, TV or games, socializing with friends. Each person finds his own way of reaching *the zone*, critical for channeling his focus.

* *Gilles Villeneuve was fatally injured during the final qualifying session for the Belgian Grand Prix in May 1982, when his car overtook a slower driver, Jochen Mass, who, spotting Villeneuve approaching behind him, shifted right to allow him to pass on the left at the same moment Villeneuve shifted to make his pass on the right.*

CHAPTER THIRTY-SEVEN

If anyone believes that motor racing is glamorous, he needs only to spend a few hours at a racetrack on a rainy day. The Indianapolis Motor Speedway provides no exception. On a cold, wet, blustery day, crews huddle together in garages, doors closed, lights blazing, awaiting respite. There is something about Indianapolis and rain. Midwestern weather patterns in May can be unpredictable. Rain is the speedway's nemesis. After only one day of track activity for the rookies, Opening Day is the first formal day of practice when everyone can get out onto the racetrack to make those first all-important laps.

In rain, track opportunity does not last long. It only takes a shower to shut down practice proceedings for an hour or two. In standing water, IndyCars cannot gain traction for running effectively. When rain occurs, everyone watches and waits. If during or preceding a race, media broadcasters divert race coverage and instead conduct driver profiles and interviews between weather updates. In the garage area, sodden fans slosh through puddles on the lookout for a driver or racing personality standing nearby who might sign an autograph or pose for a photo.

One man happy to indulge anyone who engages him is Helio Castroneves. Following his legal battle in Miami, he had returned to the cockpit to perform stronger than ever. The past several months had been debilitating; it felt great to prove that he was truly back. This he did in fine style. A seventh place finish in Long Beach and a second place finish at Kansas Speedway confirmed that he had not lost his edge. Perhaps the greatest highlight of his comeback season, however, was when Helio Castroneves stepped up to the winner's podium to claim the coveted Borg-Warner Trophy and traditional bottle of milk as the winner of the 2009 Indianapolis 500.

Castroneves' return strategy had been largely psychological: to reassemble himself, focus intently upon his driving strengths, look forward with a positive demeanor and let the negativity of recent days fall away. Having come so close to losing it all put him in touch with those things which really mattered most to him. He more fully appreciates living in the here and now. Castroneves' rebirth is evident, onlookers comment on this newly relaxed, smiling, confident man standing under his Team Penske umbrella, grabbing the microphone to interview his teammates, offer colorful commentary and joke with fans. Each aspect of this role is important to him now. Going forward, every fan, every autograph is appreciated. His story does not end here. In 2010, he continues to perform at the top of the field and remains a crowd favorite.

But, you might ask, whatever happened to the driver who temporarily filled Castroneves' seat in 2009? When Will Power stepped up to assist in Castroneves' absence, Roger Penske promised that if he performed well, Power would secure a regular seat with the team in 2010. And perform Power did, winning the pole position at Long Beach and bringing Team Penske a second place finish. He also turned in a great performance in May at the 2009 Indy 500, starting ninth and finishing in fifth place. The team entered a third car in five other races and placed Power in it. He won from the pole position at Edmonton and finished in the top 10 at the three other races.

Chapter Thirty-Seven

Debilitating back injuries suffered during a practice incident last August temporarily put Power out of commission, but sheer determination, hard work and a burning desire to race caused him to press hard through rehabilitation and emerge stronger than ever.

Roger Penske was true to his word. Now two races into the 2010 season, Power has dominated the track, securing two pole positions and two wins in the first three races of the IndyCar season, as well as a striking lead in points.

CHAPTER THIRTY-EIGHT

In 2010, IndyCar racing stands on the cusp of exciting new developments. Starting this year, IZOD has become the title sponsor of the IRL's open-wheel series, with a six-year contract (through 2016), an expansion of IZOD's former partnership with the IRL in 2008. This is the league's first title sponsor since 2001. IZOD participates in the Team Enhancement & Allocation Matrix Fund, which offers financial guarantees to race teams. The brand receives high visibility on IRL broadcasts (Versus and ABC) and is prominently advertised at IRL races, including the Indianapolis 500.

IZOD and the IRL seem to be strong, mutually-favorable alliance partners. IZOD benefits from pairing exciting traditional motorsport with lucrative advertising opportunity and high visibility for the brand within the Phillips-Van Heusen company's target market. IZOD supports IndyCar racing by advertising within deeply-entrenched retail markets beyond IndyCar's current fan base and by assisting the organization with expansive marketing/co-branding efforts within the U.S. motorsports landscape and to international markets beyond.

The 2010 Indy Racing League sees the advent of a new CEO – Randy Bernard, former CEO of The Professional Bull Riders Association for 15 years, of which he was a particularly strong marketer/promoter. Coming from outside open-wheel racing equips Bernard with a unique, external perspective and provides for out-of-the-box thinking with which to energize and expand the IndyCar brand within and beyond its existing fan base. His background in, and relationship with, network and cable television should help bring the spotlight upon a still underexposed motor sporting gem. He holds strong existing relationships with promoters and foresees co-promotional opportunities. Bernard has ample resources with which to work. The pool of talented drivers in 2010 is strong, building around interesting personalities and storylines. Any number of the top ten or fifteen might be cultivated and promoted into superstar status. Competing for the time, attention and discretionary spending of a diversified fan base, Bernard does not limit his scope to motorsporting, per se. He recognizes that IndyCar's competition encompasses anything identified as entertainment.

One challenge with which Bernard will contend is a familiar refrain – developing more American drivers to whom American audiences can relate. Add to this his intent of broadening IndyCar's fan base beyond its strongest demographic (middle-aged males) to include more women and children, and beyond its typical geography (U.S. Midwest, Canada) to woo formerly untapped regions. The Indy Grand Prix of Alabama's inaugural expansion of the series in 2010 onto a road course at Birmingham's Barber Motorsports Park is the IRL's first Southern venue, one that up until now has served as a traditional NASCAR stronghold. This may prove to be a significant move in broadening IndyCar's exposure in the domestic market.

At the same time, sustaining an international presence is good for the motor sport's financial viability, advertising visibility for team/series sponsors, and expansion of the IndyCar fan base. The largest contingent of IndyCar drivers in 2010 hails from Brazil and Apex-Brasil is a strong supporter/sponsor of this year's racing series.

Chapter Thirty-Eight

The 2010 racing season opened with The Streets of Sao Paulo, a grand prix road course throughout beautiful downtown Sao Paulo, Brazil.

In 2010, the Indy Racing League is boldly positioning the Indy 500 Race as the most prestigious and exceptional event in its racing series by broadening competitive opportunities during the qualification process.

Starting this year, at Pole Day's end, the top nine qualifiers will have their times erased and be asked to re-qualify for new rankings within one of the top nine guaranteed starting spots. Having to compete and rank twice should also ensure that the most qualified drivers on that given day are appropriately placed and rewarded. It also builds qualification into a bigger, more exciting, second event than it had been in previous years.

The four days traditionally set aside for qualification have been reduced to two – Saturday and Sunday only – now a perfect weekend event. Indy attendees will enjoy the heightened excitement of this competitive activity matching top drivers against each other – a full week before the big race.

There is much emphasis upon the pole position's reflecting the best of field for other reasons, as well. Increased cash payouts and a substantial increase in acquirable points helps to make this a standout event for competing drivers. The qualification winner will be awarded the PEAK Performance Pole Award and now $175,000 (up from $100,000 last year). The second-fastest qualifier will receive $75,000 and the third-fastest will receive $50,000.

Whereas a qualification winner formerly received one point for winning pole position, he will now receive 15 points (a dramatic increase from the one point of previous years). Going forward, lesser-ranked qualifiers will receive points, as well. Historically, they have received none. Second place will receive 13 points and third place 12. Fourth through sixth place positions will receive 11 points each. Seventh through ninth will be awarded six points each. Positions 10-24 receive four bonus points, and 25-33 earn three points each. Higher point awards provide a greater opportunity for one-off teams or partial season contenders to gain competitive strength in the series point standings as a result of their participating in the Indy 500 qualification and race.

CHAPTER THIRTY-NINE

The page may have turned, a new chapter begun, a new generation of drivers now building their own legacies, but the old dogs are still in the pound. Even the younger fans recognize them from a distance. They find themselves brushing past heroes who have made headlines and history here for more than fifty years. Significant they are, as much a part of the tradition here as the track itself.

You'll find them walking through the garage area, driving a golf cart, chatting with an acquaintance, posing for a photo, signing an autograph. Former Indy 500 winners Mario Andretti, Arie Luyenduk, Al Unser, Sr. and Al Unser, Jr. can all be seen in Gasoline Alley. These patriarchs still command respect from peers and fans, such were their achievements.

Somewhere in the speedway, you might find it – an inconspicuous door. Incongruous in its place, insignificant in appearance, yet inviting to all who pass to open it. It may appear through the mist of a cold Indianapolis night, a light from beneath casting warm glow into the empty silence. For those who dare, we open it with care, lest we release the memories within. Inside, we hear voices and laughter. Faint echoes of music emit from the basement below – Glenn Miller, Buddy Holly, Elvis Presley, Bob Dylan, The Beatles – their renderings broken intermittently by a race announcer's voice calling across the room.

A dimly lit staircase beckons. We follow it. Holding a flimsy banister, penetrating the gloom one step at a time, we descend. Through clouds of cigarette smoke, the figures are imperceptible at first. Silhouettes in a scarlet fog. But slowly their ethereal presences take shape. We stand in awe viewing what materializes before us. Over in the corner, Carl Fisher, Eddie Rickenbacker, Wilbur Shaw and Tony Hulman are playing cards. Only a fool would try to guess who holds the winning hand.

A small bar is surrounded by several familiar faces. They smile and converse with each other as old friends. There's Mauri Rose, Indy 500 winner in 1947 and 1948, chatting with fellow competitor Rex Mays. Engine guru Fred Offenhauser, looking dapper, is shoulder-to-shoulder with Louie Meyer. Huddled together are Bill Vukovich, Troy Ruttman and Johnnie Parsons.

In the shadows, beneath a neon Firestone sign, we can make out Tony Bettenhausen and Jim Rathmann. Harry Miller is doling out wisdom to a small group of latter-day heroes, among them Peter Revson, Mark Donahue, Scott Brayton, Stan Fox and Tony Renna. Gordon Smiley looks on, amused. Arthur Newby, Frank Wheeler and James Allison can be seen in animated conversation with Louis Chevrolet and Barney Oldfield. We can only imagine what they must be talking about.

And sitting alone beside a flickering lamp, casting crimson light onto his impassive features, is Eddie Sachs, victim of a fiery crash with Dave McDonald in 1964's Indy 500. There are others we can recognize – Ralph DePalma, Dario Resta, Rodger Ward, Swede Savage, Art Pollard and Lloyd Ruby, a recent inductee into this exclusive club.

The price of membership is high. But here they remain, untouched by time.

Chapter Thirty-Nine

Their laughter echoes softly through the room, absorbed by plush velvet curtains. Portraits adorn the bare brick walls, each face a faded memory to those in the world above, but here in this netherworld, they live, fed by the perennial memory of their achievements.